Homosexual Theology

Homosexual Theology

Ken Smith

iUniverse, Inc.
Bloomington

Homosexual Theology

iUniverse books may be ordered through booksellers or by contacting:

iUniverse
1663 Liberty Drive
Bloomington, IN 47403
www.iuniverse.com
1-800-Authors (1-800-288-4677)

ISBN: 978-1-4759-3826-5 (sc)
ISBN: 978-1-4759-3827-2 (e)

Printed in the United States of America

iUniverse rev. date: 07/19/2012

DEDICATION

This book is lovingly dedicated to my friends who in the world's view stand at opposite sides of a great canyon, or chasm of sexual diversity, but who with Jesus Christ as the mediator are really joined until the canyon then disappears. Though determined as homosexual and heterosexual, and lesbian those definitions disappear when the agape love, shown to us by God in his son Jesus the Christ calls us all his children, and we in turn call him our Father.

God has spoken to us in the past through his word and he continues to speak to us and deals with us as 'unique' individuals, the Holy Spirit being a constant reminder of his presence. We then seek not only to work, fellowship, and pray together but also to join in honoring God our Father by glorifying him and enjoying his presence. We look forward to his presence not only now but into the eternal future where time will not be a factor, but merely a present of presence.

We live in often unmerited grace, not only for our being in the world but also for our being children, totally loved by our Father God. We seek to understand this gift and in humility bestow and attribute any and all our honor and efforts to God the Father. We do this as a united family of God.

I appreciate the use of the New International Version of the Holy Bible for the following quotes and also the association with Dawn McAllister who ably proofs the manuscript and keeps me humble.

TABLE OF CONTENTS

FORWARD

It was soon after my thirteenth birthday that my uncle died. He left behind a wife, five children and no financial reserves. The only thing that would solve the problem of the family was to have my father drive down, pick up the entire family and move them home into our house. So, overnight our family of six became a family of twelve. There were seven boys, a baby girl, my Grandma, my Aunt and my parents. It was a tight fit.

Everything changed. We began buying food in number 10 cans, and cases of them. My father ordered a set of pottery dishes with place settings for twelve and fortunately we also got all the 'mistakes' along with the perfect plates, cups, mugs and all the rest. It became a game for us to find the imperfect plates, bowls and mugs. We looked hard and long, but to us they all seemed perfect and they seemed to last in spite of hard usage by seven growing boys.

Then my father's company ceased to exist. It had supported a larger company and when the larger company went bankrupt, so did my father's company. My mother cooked for the entire mob and our evening table was set for twelve, every night except Sunday. Then before we went to our small town Methodist Episcopal Church the table was set for thirteen, or possibly fifteen or seventeen. We could invite friends to come to Sunday dinner but we had to let mother know before church. The odd setting was for Dick Siebold, the church choir director. He would come out from the university in the neighboring city, and if no one else invited him he had dinner with us.

Following dinner and the dishes mom, who was the church's organist, and Dick sat down at our piano, a concert sized Mason Hamlin grand and we would be entertained for up to two hours with wonderful music. My mother had been headed to the concert stage before dad changed her mind. We had Brahms, Beethoven, Bach and Hayden, as well as hymns. We had them all, and with both Dick and Mom at the piano it was a rich experience. This routine continued until we had to move to another city for dad's job needs. We considered Dick a member of our family and held him in the highest of respect, as he was loved by the choir and all who knew him. He was a homosexual person.

Graduation from high school was in Pittsburgh from a school that was 90% black. I enlisted in the Army at age seventeen, the Army Specialized Training reserve program, and upon completion of six months of college work at Virginia Military Institute and Basic training in Florida I was ready to be sent to Japan for the invasion. I was deterred, however by the two atomic bombs and ended up in Germany where I supervised a personnel replacement battalion, replacing combat GIs with occupation personnel.

Upon discharge from the army I completed a college course in a small school in the Midwest with a major in psychology and accepted a position in Sitka, Alaska at Sheldon Jackson Junior College, a mission school, as dorm supervisor, athletic director and substitute teacher for three years. The fifty plus boys in the 9th and 10th grade in my dormitory during this three year assignment were from every one of the nine cultural groups in the state of Alaska.

I then completed a three year seminary course at San Francisco Theological Seminary and was appointed pastor of the Chapel by the Lake in Auke Bay, Alaska where I served for twenty two--years. As there was not much counseling available in the Juneau area, which was adjacent to Auke Bay, I had a heavy counseling load, and for a while was the counselor by direction of several of the judges in the Community in Juneau. At the time I also served the state of Alaska on the 1202 Commission, the Post-Secondary Commission overseeing all post-secondary and proprietary schools.

My next place of service was in Hawai'i on the Island of Kaua'i at Waimea where I served for twelve years. My charge was to form a cooperation parish of Japanese, Hawaiian and Haole (English Speaking) folks as the Waimea Parish. I also served in the Kaua'i Mokupuni (association) and also as Vice President and then President for the Hawai'i Conference of the United Church of Christ. Again there was much counseling, and I also served the state of Hawai'i on the State Health Planning and Developmental Agency. This agency oversaw all medical work, institutions and medical needs for each of the island counties and also for the hospitals in Honolulu. I served on the Sub Area Council for Kaua'i, then on the state board as chair of the Certificate of Need Committee and finally as the president of the state wide council for SHPDA.

My final professional service was in Eagle River, Alaska, adjacent to Anchorage, as the pastor of the Presbyterian Church that was a mission but became self-supporting. Though counseling was again a major responsibility I was also involved through the church in the food bank, Alcoholics Anonymous which had a room in the church dedicated to AA, and finally as the folks of the congregation created a Prostitute Habilitation program in Anchorage, I was a member of the board that came to be known as the Mary Magdalene Project Alaska.

Building projects were completed at each location and these were accomplished by volunteer labor of the members of the congregations. Again counseling was considerable. Upon retirement I wrote a book "Dick and Jane" for pre-marriage folks that also contains an outline for five sessions of pre-marriage counseling. I have been involved in over 6000 counseling sessions. In each of my congregations I have had homosexual folks, some openly and others, "don't ask and don't tell" and I've done extensive counseling with them, as well as heterosexual counseling.

I am heterosexual, but I have many friends and family who are homosexual. Homosexual and lesbian folks were members of every one of the congregations that I have served. They are wonderful folks, with sparkling Christian lives who are a definite plus to the community. So when I consider the great debate that has yet to settle down about the "wrongness" of homosexuality as against the "rightness" of heterosexuality, I confess to being confused. As Mother Theresa has said and I believe applies to homosexuals, "If you cannot love the person you see, how can you love God, whom you cannot see"?

It is with this background that I determined to find out what the Bible really says about sexuality, or what it does not say, and the following is the result of my finding and thinking. Please note that I have intentionally used a format where there is extra space that you can use to note any questions or comments that might come to mind as you read. Rather than making notes on a separate piece of paper, where they can be misplaced or lost, your thoughts easily can be found because they are there with the material that suggested them.

INTRODUCTION

For conservatives, homosexuality is a controversial and volatile subject because they have decided that homosexuals have chosen a way of life that is considered sinful and immoral. When it comes to choice, however, I have counseled with many homosexual individuals and not one says that they would choose that particular stand if they had a choice. As Bishop Desmond Tutu of South Africa has said, "Few people would choose a path that is so difficult in so many cultures . . . a path that can lead to vilification, even murder." It is something that is thrust upon them, and only when they admit it and usually find a partner, do they find peace in their life situation. Fortunately, extensive scientific research has begun to answer the question of what homosexuality is. Is it genetic? Is it a choice? Or is it environmental?

It also is important to recognize that during the past 100 years, there have been several scientific studies into what determines a person's sexual orientation. Various studies by psychiatrists, and various counseling and medical attempts to change the sexual orientation of homosexuals have all led current research to look into biological, hormonal, and genetic causes. Science, of course is not my area of expertise, so for more information on this information, there are many articles on the internet about the projects and their success in proving a biological connection to homosexuality. They can be found by looking up "science and homosexuality."

While science is definitely pointing to a biological basis for sexual orientation, however, there is an even more powerful force at work and reason to accept these people for who and what they are, and that is the focus of this book.

Who or what is a homosexual person? Almost all people accept the fact that when they come into the Junior High age that they will be affected by the maleness or femaleness of those around them, usually being attracted by the sexuality of those who are of the opposite sex. It is natural to be affected by a person of the opposite sex. However, there are folks, perhaps five to ten percent of the population, who are not affected by this supposedly normal feeling, but are naturally instead attracted to others of their own sexual orientation: girls affected by other girls and boys affected by other boys.

These persons are homosexual folks, or at least tend to be homosexual. With some, the normal orientation takes place a little later and they continue on with normal heterosexual feelings. With the majority displaying these feelings those with normal homosexual feelings wonder why they are 'different', but for them their sexual feelings are natural and normal. They were born with those feelings inherent in their psyche and only later were they discovered when puberty was achieved.

There are some who feel that the heterosexual feelings are the only natural feelings and therefore have devised ways of 'tricking' the personality into a different sexuality. There is a great question over whether or not they are successful and also whether or not it is good for the sexual orientation to be tricked in such a manner. Let's also be aware of the fact that many of the sacred writings were in print before a thorough understanding of sexuality was determined.

Science has yet to discover why some persons are homosexual while others are heterosexual. There are a very few who are bisexual or transvestite, where their sexuality swings between homosexual and heterosexual.

Often the feeling of being different can be frightening, particularly when they are expected to be normally heterosexual, but they know they are different. All of us, even fraternal twins are different persons and to be different is to be normal. We are not produced by an assembly line where the 'different' person is thrown on the rejection pile. To be different is to be wonderful.

In this treatise I shall not use the slang names for the 'Gay' community, believing that all is not happiness in the homosexual community. Likewise I will not use the word 'straight' for those who are heterosexual, realizing that first it implies that the homosexual is not straight and second that many in the ultraconservative or pseudo conservative community could really be considered crooked in their actions, their words and their intents. As our church emphases and denominational branches are becoming more and more transparent, we have realized that openness and not secretiveness is very important. Decisions that we made and make are not just for time but for eternity. Possibly only as we grow older do we realize the importance of this.

The purpose of this writing is to put down my thoughts so that I can compare them in the light of the present Twentieth Century concepts with the Biblical standards; that have not changed since, with the Holy Spirit the writers put them down in words, so that I can make personal changes according to what the Bible says. You will soon realize, however that I'm looking for theological answers in scripture. I am looking for Biblical answers. In a sense, I want the Bible to prove what it really says about homosexuality. I trust the Bible and also the Holy Spirit's explanation and inspiration.

For those unfamiliar with the Bible, and who confuse it with possibly other supposedly religious sacred works, let me relate an experience again found on the internet. During a question and answer session at a recent speaking engagement, a university student asked, "Why do you believe that the

Bible is the inspired word of God?" What is so special, so unique about the Bible that Christians believe it is literally the inspired word of God? The speaker in answering the questioner suggested the following. "First, the Bible is not just one single book. This is a more common misconception than many people realize, especially with people who do not come from a Judeo-Christian background. Rather than being a single book, the Bible is actually a collection of 66 books, which is called the canon of scriptures. These 66 books contain a variety of genres: history, poetry, prophecy, wisdom literature. They contain general letters and apocalyptic writings, just to name a few.

"Second, these 66 books were written by 40 different authors. These authors came from a variety of backgrounds: shepherds, fishermen, doctors, kings, prophets, and others. And most of these authors never knew one another personally.

"Third, these 66 books were written over a period of 1500 years. Yet, again, this is another reminder that many of these authors never knew or collaborated with one another in writing these books.

"Fourth, the 66 books of the Bible were written in 3 different languages. In the Bible we have books that were written in the ancient languages of Hebrew, Greek, and Aramaic; a reflection of the historical and cultural circumstances in which each of these books were written.

"And finally, these 66 books were written on 3 different continents: Africa, Asia, and Europe, once again, a testament to the varied historical and cultural circumstances of God's people and this collection of books shares a common storyline—the creation, fall and redemption of God's people : a common theme—God's universal love for all of humanity; and a common message—salvation is available to all who repent of their sins and commit to following God with all of their heart, soul, mind and strength."

It would be helpful to mention that the Christian has an aid in the reading of the Bible. As the Holy Spirit assists in the writing of the Bible so also does the Holy Spirit assist in the reading of the Bible.That means that when you read the Bible the Holy Spirit brings your mind up to date to read in light of the modern culture of which you are a part to often bring meaning that would otherwise be lost. This keeps you up to date in the culture of which you are a part and gives you wisdom in that culture and often gives you strength to change the culture for the betterment of society.

Other supposed non-Christian scriptures take the reader back anywhere from ten to fourteen-hundred years, and you have to make the transition yourself without God's help. And, often there is not enough information given to give you an honest or accurate concept of the writer's intention.

It would be wise to digress at this point to understand a little more about the Bible. Several homosexual folk have said that they question whether or not the Bible is valid for them as the Christians who oppose them take their doctrines from the Bible. So it would be wise to understand the book, or books of the Bible.

Every Christian pastor has or should have a Hebrew Old Testament and a Greek New Testament in his or her private library. Let's look at the Hebrew Old Testament. On the cover mine says, "Biblia Hebraica, Edidit Rudolf Kittel," which means it is the Hebrew Bible with the editor Rudolf Kittel. However when you open the book, a rather large tome, you find that you are at the end of the Old Testament. Inside the back cover is the beginning of the Old Testament. Hebrew is written from right to left and the Bible begins at what we would call the back end of the book.

As you open the book you note the strange Hebrew letters, beginning on the right hand side of the page and all sorts of dots and dashes over, under and in the middle of the Hebrew letters. The letters you see are Hebrew but they are consonants. The dots and dashes are Hebrew vowels. Then note that there are two columns with the Hebrew letters and consonants at the top. Below are lots of Hebrew, or Greek or Latin or English, writings. These are the places where the Hebrew either connects with the Greek New Testament, or is a reference to sources for the texts.

Every manuscript or parchment with a small or large amount of writing is included. Biblical scholars can match just about any phrase with its correct place in the canon, the body of scripture, and just a dot (jot or tittle) can make a difference. (Matthew 5:18) This is of course true in English, whether sat, set, sit, sot, or sut, just by changing the vowel, which to the Hebrew is the dot or dash. In some cases there are words missing so the missing word depends upon what is before and after it. [Sometimes there are words that are bracketed] These words are not in the Hebrew or Greek texts but are included in order to make sense of the passage in which they are written. As you read, your eye skips over the bracket but if you are conscious of them then they will appear.

Occasionally there are small letters attached to a phrase or word of the text. At the bottom of the page you will find the letters with an accompanying word of explanation or else a reference to some other place where the words are also duplicated. Once you are immersed in the study of the language you can feel your way through the thoughts and they make great sense.

Let's look at the <u>Greek New Testament</u>, edited by Kurt Aland, Matthew Black, Bruce M. Metzger and Allen Wikgren, the text by D. Eb Nestle. Again, as in the Hebrew Old Testament, you have the text at the top of the page but under it usually separated by a line are all sorts of letters, Greek, sometimes Hebrew and also English. These indicate the source, or from which place the passage came. We have none of the original texts or manuscripts which constitute the original writings. There is a small card on which is listed the codices (Code, such as Hamurabi), the editors related to the manuscripts and signs and abbreviations used. We believe that the Holy Spirit worked with and through the original authors and also works in and through you as you read the Bible, helping you to understand it and also to effect changes in your life on the authority of the Bible. You should have access to a commentary as well as a concordance and possibly a good Bible dictionary.

The translation, therefore, is taking the Hebrew and Greek and putting it into English, German, Latin or other, language. When the missionaries went to Hawai'i, they did not translate from the English Bible; but rather from the Hebrew and Greek into the Hawaiian language. If one translates from a translation then it is a 'paraphrase'. Many modern pastors prefer to use a paraphrase, but check occasionally with the original sources. One large Christian denomination has a Bible that they translated from the Latin rather than the Greek and Hebrew as the Latin strengthens their theological stands.

In many cases in the modern vernacular there is not a similar word to the Greek, Hebrew or modern translation, so new translations are written using modern phraseology. This is important as in the Bible there are words that are either untranslatable or which carry many different meanings. When I mention this, think back to this discussion, for it makes a great difference. For instance, there is no word in Hebrew for homosexual and the long term partner relationships that most homosexual folks enjoy in this day and age, relationships which they wish to formalize in a church or state rite of marriage. Such a word is unknown to the writers of the original manuscripts of the Bible. There is no such word in the Bible languages for the relationship did not exist in Bible times. Though, we will see that some relationships did exist, just without a name.

There are three forms of government that exist under the authority of the Bible. They are Hierarchial, Presbyterian and Congregational. I have been involved with all three in one way or another. I was raised for fifteen years, and made a confession of Faith in Jesus Christ as my Lord and Savior in the Methodist Episcopal Church, a hierarchal expression where the power and authority comes down from the Bishop, to the District Superintendent to the pastors and then the lay folk. Others are the Roman Catholic with power coming down from the Pope, to cardinals, bishops and priests, and also the Episcopal, with power coming down from bishops.

I became a Presbyterian in the United Presbyterian, Scottish Covenanter denomination, went to seminary and have served in the Presbyterian denomination. However I also served for 15 years in the United Church of Christ, a congregational relationship, where the power comes up from the congregation then to the Associations; with members of the congregations and pastors involved and then the Conference. Finally there is the Presbyterian system with pastors and lay folk involved in the local congregation, the Presbytery, the Synod (soon to be changed) and the General Assembly. All three forms of church government have Christian folk that theologically go from liberal to highly conservative with many different positions in between and that cover many different facets of the congregational worship. All Christian denominations are one of these three types of church government, involving lay folk within church government.

OLD TESTAMENT THEOLOGICAL BIBLICAL MUSINGS ON HOMOSEXUALITY

The Bible says, "The chief end of man is to glorify God and enjoy him forever." That is the first question in the shorter Westminster Catechism of the Presbyterian Church and in God's word, and it guides all that follows. That means that the purpose of ALL mankind, woman and man, and ALL races, colors and even theological bents have as their purpose to do that which glorifies God and makes him (her) happy. The homosexual individual is not excluded. Therefore that which we, regardless of which community we are a part, do to glorify God and to help every other individual to glorify God is important, again regardless of which community we are a part. If we keep someone from glorifying God, if we stand between that person and God with a negative attitude then we are not benefitting that individual or God, and we are sinning. Of course we can all spell "sin" and we should note that the letter in the middle is "I". Again, I am reminded that the stand of the conservative that homosexuality is a choice of the individual has been pretty much scientifically disproven. At the present time there is no clear answer as to how an individual comes to claim himself, or herself as homosexual or lesbian.

I have talked and counseled with many homosexual individuals and not one says that they would choose that particular stand if they had a choice. It is something that is thrust upon them at their birth, and only when they admit it and usually find a partner do they find peace in their life situation. To deny them the opportunity to live a full life that glorifies God again comes up sounding like sin.

Possibly a word of explanation is in place here. I have pastored five congregations, two single congregations and a parish of three churches, Japanese, Hawaiian and haole, which means foreigner and usually refers to Caucasian. I have had homosexual persons in all of the congregations that I have served, some that were known to the rest of the congregation and others who chose not to reveal their sexual orientation. They have been welcomed folks, active in the life of the church and active in the life of the community. We have been and are good friends and that covers the period of my ministry and also retirement. I have never asked a person who wished to make a confession of faith in Jesus Christ as Lord and savior, and therefore wished to become a member of a congregation that I served, whether he or she was homosexual or heterosexual.

My first homosexual counseling relationship was with an individual who was put in jail because of his homosexuality. He had done nothing wrong but his religious group felt that he was sinful and he was jailed until someone realized that there was no law against homosexuality. It was an intensive and extensive listening and learning experience. He had much to say.

Most of the homosexual persons that I have known had or have a partner, some were relatively new in their relationship and a few were celebrating over sixty years of being together, were respected folks in the community and were deemed some of the best workers that their employers had ever hired, and some were excellent state workers.

Before we begin the Biblical record let us digress for a moment to the Code of Hammurabi. It is a code of conduct dating to 1780, B. C. possibly the oldest writing of a legal code in the world. It is a Babylonian law code that Hammurabi, who was the sixth Babylonian King, enacted to let the people of his kingdom know how to act. The code consists of 282 laws, with appropriate punishments if they were broken.

A nearly complete example of the Code is still surviving on a diorite stele in the shape of a huge index finger. As a Christian I would like it to point up to God, but probably it was in the form of an index finger wagging before the people telling them to be good. The Stele is about seven and a half feet high and the code is inscribed in the Akkadian language, using cuneiform script, carved into the stele.

There were, and still are, clay tablets with some of the laws inscribed on them, sort of an early iPad, Babylonian style. If you wished to use it a second time then you mudded it over and carved a new set of laws. Within the code are all sorts of legal provisions: the liability of a builder for a house that he built but which collapses, family relationships such as inheritance, divorce, paternity and other sexual behavior.

However, there is no indication in any of the 282 laws concerning homosexuality. There are several laws concerning military service and behavior. Some of the laws evidently leaked into parts of the 613 laws that came after the Ten Commandments, though these laws were for the Babylonian King, while we will find that the Ten Commandments are from and for God and his people.

GENESIS

In the 27th verse of the first chapter of Genesis we read, "So God created man (kind) in his own image, in the image of God he created him; male and female he created them." And then in the 31st verse it reads, "God saw all that he had made, and it was very good. And there was evening and there was morning – the sixth day." There was no reference to homosexual or lesbian folk being bad, nor did God say that 95% of what he created was good or even that 90% of all he created was good. Instead he said 100 % of all he created was good.

Possibly it would be good to examine the word "good" as it is used here and in other parts of scripture. It is an adjective, though at times can be used as a noun and is the Hebrew word *tob* which is found about 559 times in the Hebrew Old Testament. It denotes good in every sense of that word. Various meanings are festive, favorable, pleasant, right, best, delightful. It is good to remember that the creation of each individual was "good" in God's sight. It is good to begin to realize that God's Word is good for God's will. Often we question how we fit in, but always the good is for or on behalf of God.

I recognize that the heterosexual community says that only about 5% of the population is homosexual while the homosexual community says that there are 10% homosexuals within the general population. Again, God saw all that he had created and it was all good. I believe that God is continually involved in creation, and that the creation that he effects today is likewise 100% good. The Greek language brings that out best through the "imperfect tense", which means a continuing action. Everything that is created involves God, whether he directly creates it or gives the opportunity to others to create. As he is still creating people, and as far as we can tell the percentage of the population is still the same at either 5% or 10% homosexual, God must still feel that they are good.

There are many attributes that we credit to god; that he is omniscient, omnipotent, all powerful, all knowing and the lists goes on and also includes all consistent. God has not changed, though our understanding of him may have changed. As humans we find that there are many things that we did not know and through study we have new understandings, but God's wisdom is unchanging.

Another mention that the Word has about homosexuals is found in the story of Lot, (Genesis, chapters 18 and 19) who chooses with his family to live in the valley or plain of Sodom and Gomorrah along with those who are homosexual, and the visitation of angels. In support of their stand against homosexuality, many Christians like to use this story of Sodom and Gomorrah.

First let us look at the 20th & following verses of the 18th chapter. The Lord has heard the outcry; against Sodom and Gomorrah and has determined to destroy them. "The outcry against Sodom and Gomorrah is so great and their sin so grievous that I will go down and see if what they have done is as bad as the outcry that has reached me. If not, I will know." There then follows a verbal sparring between Abraham asking the Lord not to destroy Sodom if there are righteous people there. In support of their stand against homosexuality many Christians like to use this story of Sodom and Gomorrah. This will be further discussed under Ezekiel.

Let's now look at God and his creation. He created many people throughout the world, and they were not all, of the Jewish lineage. His will, we believe, was to separate a special people who would bring all the others into God's Kingdom. It would take a while for the Jews to realize this, and accept it; and one wonders if they, or we the Christian children of the faith, even realize it today. God, therefore, made hospitality a strong point in the Jewish faith. For those who are not of the faith, but who are poor and needy, God's people were to be benevolent, and still must be today.

Carefully reading the passage today we realize that God was not overly concerned with the homosexual folks, more or less than with the others so he provided in the Hebrew religion a means of taking care of those needy throughout the world. Even today the needs of the world call forth the benevolence of God's people and those who inherited the Judeo-Christian faith pattern. The people of Sodom did not measure up. One does wonder if we, an obese and overweight culture measure up today. But there are still many that feel that the only sin, in spite of Ezekiel, is that of homosexuality.

We should be aware of the fact that there is no Hebrew word for "homosexual". Though the concept and fact of homosexuality may have existed, there is no word for the state of being of the homosexual. Homosexual persons are considered part of the population and to designate them it is necessary to describe their actions. It is hard to describe their thoughts and self-concepts. The practice must have been wide-spread, though, as Lot was evidently living, peacefully with them in the plain cities.

In essence the angels come to visit lot and the homosexual folk of the city ask that Lot give the angels to the homosexual men supposedly for their sexual pleasure and Lot refuses to do it. Lot even offers his daughters, which he realizes that they probably will not accept. The result is fire and brimstone on the Sodom and Gomorrah folks, and the resulting feeling that whenever fire and brimstone is mentioned in the Bible somewhere before, during or after the event homosexual folk will be involved, at least in people's thinking. This is the story that we have heard time and again and supposedly proves that all homosexual persons are at fault.

As we have viewed this story many times in many different contexts, I have the feeling that possibly I am not seeing, and have not seen the essence of what the story teaches. Let me digress for a moment for I am reminded of two pictures that we have in our home.

We have many pictures on the walls of our home, not of the great masters but of places and things that bring back memories of our life lived in Alaska and Hawai'i. Two of the pictures are troublesome because they are wrong. Visitors, not knowing too much of our family history, are thrilled when they see these pictures but it bothers those of us who are totally familiar with life in Alaska.

One picture is of a Grumman Goose aircraft flying through the snow covered mountains cutting through a pass. It is an excellent picture, depicts many travels that we made in a Grumman Goose aircraft, but it is a false picture. There were two airlines that preceded Alaska Airlines in Southeastern Alaska; Ellis Airlines and Alaska Coastal Airlines. The Ellis

Air planes were painted with orange and light green, almost chartreuse. Alaska Coastal planes were painted blue with a wide yellow stripe down the side and across the wing. The picture hanging on our wall is of a plane painted orange and blue, which neither airline would have accepted as they were in competition. As we look at the picture our eyes are continually drawn to the wrong colors. I can still remember the many times that I took off sitting in the co-pilot's seat and the pilot would reach up with his right hand and adjust the engines' pitch. It is a wonderful memory.

The other picture is a pen and ink depiction of the Chapel that I served for twenty two years, the trees around it, and then the Auke Lake immediately in front of the Chapel with the shores around the lake. There are the right number of logs in the picture of the log Chapel. The immediate trees are accurately depicted and the scene is as we saw it for twenty-two years.

However, the artist evidently painted from a slide of the chapel for when she got around to painting the Mendenhall Glacier and the mountain range behind it and the snow field she put the slide in backwards so that a part of the glacier turns to the right of the mountain while in reality it turns to the left of the mountain. There is no snow field to the right of the mountain, so the picture is an impossible scene.

The picture really looks fine except for those who are familiar with the terrain and the error calls attention to the falseness of the painting. Those who are unfamiliar are impressed and yet we who are more familiar with the view, having seen it for twenty-two years are depressed. Let us look more carefully at the picture of Lot and the homosexual folk in Gomorrah. At first glance, it looks okay to us, but it is wrong. We are seeing the wrong thing. You have been told something and that thought, on the basis of those words, keeps you from possibly seeing what is really there.

Let's look at the picture of the angels, the homosexuals and the resulting displeasure of God. First I would suggest that God is more concerned with verbs than he is with nouns. Yes, nouns are important, the world is made up of them, and God has created them. But how those nouns react, the verbal part of the sentence, is possibly of more import. I feel that God's displeasure is aimed at the <u>actions</u> of the homosexual folk rather than at the homosexual folk themselves. God's anger is that they are forcing their sexual orientation on to others who do not share their orientation.

The anger of God is not at the fact of homosexuality, which he has created, but on the actions of the homosexual folk in this incident, as though in some way God made a mistake when he created homosexual and lesbian folk. This is a difficult thing to consider because the heterosexual folk, in this modern age, are engaged often in trying to change the sexual orientation of the homosexual folks around them.

And, well meaning folk are still trying to find a 'sure way' to change those who are satisfied, finally, with their sexual orientation, to something that is foreign to their orientation. In essence what we are saying is that God was wrong to have those "other" sexual folks and we need to change them. I wonder if God is happy, now when we go to great lengths to attempt to change the sexual orientation of modern homosexual folk.

But Genesis 18 and 19 is a very problematic passage. It hinges on the Hebrew word *yada,* which most conservative commentators define as "know" and is problematic because the word *yada* is used in the Bible only ten times as "know" as a sexual term. Nine hundred and thirty times in the Bible it has a different definition. It is also used in the form of "to know," and therefore to be suspicious of the strangers, as though they were spies and possibly they wanted to know about the city so that they might attack the city which the Sodomites needed to safe--guard.

Or is it possible that the Lord brings down his wrath because the people of Sodom are not hospitable to strangers, as we have just seen? They do not practice charity, which means not being aware of folks who are poor. To help strangers was a solemn religious duty, as mentioned in Leviticus 19:33-34 and Matthew 25:35, 38, and 43. There were many laws that guaranteed the strangers' safe--keeping within the Hebrew community, even if they were not of the community.

This seems to be the situation in Ezekiel 16:49, 50 where it states, "Now this was the sin of your sister Sodom: She and her daughters were arrogant and over fed and unconcerned; they did not help the poor and needy. They were haughty and did detestable things before me. Therefore I did away with them as you have seen." This then gives the reader several possibilities, whether the desire of the Sodomites was to rape the angels, who were not as human beings; or to be involved in homosexual actions and relationships or possibly to be uncharitable to those who needed help in order to live. It was a serious thing to not give help when you had resources and there were neighbors who needed help in order to live.

EXODUS

We enter now the legal part of the life of the Israelites, with the issuing of the Ten Commandments. The people have been in Egypt for a long time and have developed a slave mentality while there. It will take a lot of urging on the part of Moses and Aaron, and eventually plagues, to release the children of Israel to cross the Red Sea and begin their wandering, ultimately to find a land that they can call their own, determined by God. Stubbornness is a hard thing to overcome. A body at rest stays at rest or it takes a lot of effort to help it move. It is necessary for Moses to climb a mountain and have God issue the Ten Commandments in order for the folk to be a large family of God, the precursors of the future when all mankind will be in the family of God. The Ten Commandments, from Exodus 20:3-17 are:

1. You shall have no other gods before me.

2. You shall not make for yourself an idol in the form of anything in heaven above or on the earth beneath or in the waters below. You shall not bow down to them or worship them: for I the Lord your God am a jealous God punishing the children for the sin of the fathers to the third and fourth generation of those who hate me, but showing love to a thousand generations of those who love me and keep my commandments.

3. You shall not misuse the name of the Lord your God, for the Lord will not hold anyone guiltless who misuses his name.

4. Remember the Sabbath day by keeping it holy. Six days you shall labor and do all your work, but the seventh day is a Sabbath to the Lord your God. On it you shall not do any work, neither you, nor your son or daughter, nor your manservant or maid servant, nor your animals, nor the alien within your gates. For in six days the Lord made the heavens and the earth, the sea and all that is in them but rested on the seventh day. Therefore the Lord blessed the Sabbath day and made it holy.

5. Honor your father and your mother, so that you may live long in the land the Lord God is giving you.

6. You shall not murder.

7. You shall not commit adultery.

8.   You shall not steal.

9.   You shall not give false testimony against your neighbor.

10. You shall not covet your neighbor's house. You shall not covet your neighbor's wife, or his manservant or his maidservant, his ox or donkey or anything that belongs to your neighbor.

The first four commandments have to do with the Hebrews and their relationship to God, the one God, and then the rest of the commandments have to do with the daily living of the people who will be God's family. They involve parents, murder, adultery, false testimony, and coveting various persons or things. Nowhere in the commandments given by God is there anything specifically to do with homosexuality. This will only be introduced by man in the legal system that supposedly works the Ten Commandments into 613 laws that govern the people and that also are the basis for establishing formal family life in the Jewish community.

Early and often the children of Israel are told to have children, large families to fill the earth. Nor was it just the Israelites, for all cultures wanted to grow large and family life was how they would do it. Of course the homosexual person of the day, was not involved in having children. There is a reason that the religious leaders of the day were not happy with homosexual relationships. They did not produce more children. This is being written in October of 2011. On the 31st of this month the world will have its 7 billionth person born. It could be said that we have filled the earth; but unfortunately though the earth can still feed its people it is reaching a point where not all the people born can find sufficient food. Many Third World people live in arid areas that cannot produce enough food to sustain the population, while those areas that can produce the food are a long and expensive transportation system away from the people in need. We also face the fact that with changing weather patterns aridity is more a fact of life than ever before. Water will soon be more important than oil.

LEVITICUS

The Biblical book of Leviticus is the Old Testament's legal tome. Many theologians feel it puts in practicality the Ten Commandments, at least the parts that have to do with family living. After all, we are working at establishing a family of God to ultimately live with God in an eternal worshipful relationship and these laws and interpretations of laws are supposed to be the guidance system for one becoming a part of the family of God. We show love to God, whose people we are, by keeping his commandments. The commandments in Leviticus are the means of showing that love.

When the children of Israel left for the exile it was necessary to have some code of living and the 613 laws were that code, established by the priests and ultimately put down in the book of Leviticus. However many of these laws do not relate directly to or from the Ten Commandments. The 613 laws are not direct descendants of the Ten Commandments. Foremost in the minds of the priests was the fact that they were building a family of God that would have to endure in the midst of foreign nations that had multiple gods with varying codes of conduct, and worship ideas that were totally foreign to the Children of Israel. The priests who were contributing material were returning from the exile, along with priests that had not taken part in the exile. Both often used lists of rules that were found in differing areas. As the book of Leviticus has a consistent form of writing, it is apparent that the rules found there were often borrowed from other transitions and incorporated into God's word. Leviticus, chapters 17 to 26 are known as the Holiness Code as there is an excessive use of the word "holy."

This is not bad, but it should be kept in mind when considering the 613 rules. They were not all derivatives from the Ten Commandments, but rather were rules that priests had discovered in other areas and from other traditions. God can be allowed to work in those traditions also, but remember that we are dealing with the primary fact of the Love of God. We know of no known study that would determine from where each individual rule was derived, but the Book of Leviticus is the first known assembling of such rules, following the Code of Hammurabi while at the same time giving God the credit for establishing the rules. Always these rules were to lead to that process and ultimate end.

Specifically let's look at Leviticus 18:22. Which says: "You shall not lie with a man as with a woman; that is an abomination." First it says nothing of two women and it is in force because it is a 'violation of nature', not a violation of God's law. Whereas the other sexual sins in this 18th chapter are each given with a reason for the rule, there is none given for this violation. In addition, if the person has been created with a homosexual nature, then is it a violation of that, or their nature?

The knowledge of homosexuality was much different in those days than is our knowledge of DNA and other gene possibilities which is now common knowledge. Even today we have yet to determine why some, possibly 10 % of the population are homosexual, but we do know that they are different. And is this so strange? Each individual of the 7 billion presently on the earth is different, whether it is due to culture, or color of skin, or size of body. We are not manufactured as robots so that all think alike, act alike, have identical desires and are alike, or rejected at the time of manufacture.

As it is, if there are two identical persons born, we spend our time looking for those things that make them different from each other. If the bodies are the same then the search is deeper into the quality or the personality of the two persons. God is glorified when we use the differences in our lives to honor and glorify him. Often in pre-marriage counseling the couple will look for those differences in background, or perception or personality that will make for an interesting marriage rather than to have two persons who think alike and really try to be alike. But we must again stress that our purpose is to glorify God and enjoy him forever, each one of the seven billion inhabitants. This is now being written on the 31st of October 2011 which is the day on which the seven billionth person is born. She is a little girl in the Philippine Islands.

But this passage is part of the Holiness Law and there were many other things involved. Other parts of these laws are no longer valid, such as freedom to wear a tattoo, to eat rare meat or pork, to wear blends of different kinds of cloth, or seed their fields with different kinds of seeds and even get a haircut. Only the part that deals with homosexuality it seems is still valid.

RUTH

There are two situations, and possibly others found in scripture which speak to the close relationship that persons have who are of the same sexual orientation. They are relationships that exist in the continuum of scripture and so I introduce them because of the order of the books in which they are found. The first is a relationship between Ruth and Naomi in the book of Ruth. It is a short book, only a few pages and I'd ask you to read it rather than quoting the entire passage here. It involves Naomi who lives in Moab, a foreign country, with her husband Elimelech. She has two sons that are married to Moabites and then Elimelech and the sons, die.

If the men had died in their native country, there would be provision for the widows to be taken care of. Hebrew law was good on this point, but that law did not exist outside the boundaries of the country. Naomi decides to return to her native Israel and Ruth determines to go with her, abandoning her own country to be with Naomi.

It is harvest time and Ruth suggests that she go follow the harvesters and glean grain. She finds herself in the field of Boaz, a cousin of her father-in-law. He is a kinsman-redeemer, with the result that following the customary procedure he and Ruth are married and have a son, Obed who became the father of Jesse, the father of David.

The verse that stands out, uttered when Naomi decides to return to Israel and suggests that Ruth return to her own land, is in Ruth 1:16 ,17, But Ruth replied, "Don't urge me to leave you or to turn back from you. Where you go I will go, and where you I stay I will stay. Your people will be my people and your God my God. Where you die I will die, and there I will be buried. May the Lord deal with me, be it ever so severely, if anything but death separates you and me."

So it is that Ruth and Naomi continue their relationship, which is in no way a deterrent to the relationship between Ruth and Boaz. It is a relationship that many women have today with a soul-mate of the same sex. God honors these relationships as they live their lives preparing to spend eternity with God the Father, possibly because of the relationship making deeper their relationship with God the Father.

SAMUEL

The second listing of a great mutual love in a same sex situation is between David and Jonathan, the first son of Saul, and therefore the probable successor to be the king of Israel upon Saul's death. In the story David has been selected to be the hero in killing Goliath, using his shepherding skills to kill the giant, but at the same time gaining a great deal of notoriety. This leads to a great Jealousy by Saul, the first king of the Israelites.

"After David had finished talking with Saul, Jonathan became one in spirit with David, and he loved him as himself. From that day Saul kept David with him and did not let him return to his father's house. And Jonathan made a covenant with David because he loved him as himself. Jonathan took off the robe he was wearing and gave it to David, along with his tunic, and even his sword, his bow and his belt. (I Samuel 18:1-4)

In I Samuel 20th, chapter King Saul seeks David with the intent to kill him. Jonathan, Saul's first son and a close friend of David still is not sure of Saul's feelings so sets up a means of determining how his father views David and then how he can warn David. If Saul shows anger toward David Jonathan will warn him, through shooting arrows in a field. If Jonathan tells his servant boy that the arrows are beyond him, then the anger is real and David's life will continually be in jeopardy. If the arrows fall short then David is safe to return to the palace to his appointed place.

Saul does show anger and attempts to kill Jonathan and so the following day the arrows are beyond the servant boy, who collects them and then returns to the town. (I Samuel 40:40 – 42) "Then Jonathan gave his weapons to the boy and said 'Go, carry them back to town.' After the boy had gone, David got up from the south side [of the stone] and bowed down before Jonathan three times, with his face to the ground. Then they kissed each other and wept together--but David wept the most.

"Jonathan said to David, 'Go in peace for we have sworn friendship with each other in the name of the Lord, saying 'the Lord is witness between you and me, and between your descendants and my descendants forever'. Then David left, and Jonathan went back to the town."

Later, when Saul and Jonathan have been killed David's lament (II Samuel 1:25—27) is "How the mighty have fallen in battle! Jonathan lies slain on your heights. I grieve for you, Jonathan my brother; you were very dear to me. Your love for me was wonderful, more wonderful than that of women. How the mighty have fallen! The weapons of war have perished."

David's love for Jonathan extended even further for when the fighting was over in II Samuel 9:1, 6, 7 "David asked, 'is there anyone still left of the houses of Saul to whom I can show kindness for Jonathan's sake?' When Mephibosheth son of Jonathan, the son of Saul, came to David he bowed down to pay him honor. David said, 'Mephibosheth'. 'Your servant,' he replied, 'Don't be afraid,' David said to him. 'For, I will surely show you kindness for the sake of your father Jonathan. I will restore to you all the land that belonged to your grandfather, Saul, and you will always eat at my table.'"

We have found in normal discussions and also in counseling sessions the close relationships that are parallel to that closeness that David and Jonathan experienced. This closeness, also found in heterosexual marriage relationships is the basis for strength when anchored in a closer--ness to God and His will for their lives. This closeness is perhaps parallel to the closeness that the disciples felt for Jesus and accounts for their willingness to head out into the world, even if singly, geographically singing his praises.

ISAIAH

For many of the expositors of the Old Testament, the minute that Sodom and Gomorrah are mentioned the thoughts immediately come in that there are homosexual individuals involved. In the first chapter of Isaiah 1:2-4. we read, "Hear, O heavens! Listen, O earth! For the Lord has spoken: 'I reared children and brought them up, but they have rebelled against me. The ox knows his master, the donkey his owner's manger, but Israel does not know, my people do not understand'. Ah, sinful nation, a people loaded with guilt, a brood of evil doers, children given to corruption! They have forsaken the Lord; they have spurned the Holy one of Israel and turned their backs on him."

The prophet lists a long list of sins showing that the people of Israel have rebelled against God, lacking in knowing God, with idolatry, and depending upon meaningless religious ritual. The list continues: Being unjust and oppressive to others, and being totally insensitive to the needs of widows and orphans, even committing murder, accepting bribes along with other sins. Nowhere in the entire chapter is there a mention of homosexuality but the commentator, seeing the Sodom and Gomorra reference of punishment will include homosexuality and other sexual promiscuous activities.

A further comment is in order. There are many passages in English Bibles which clearly condemn same-sex activities but when the original Greek or Hebrew texts are studied they are unrelated to homosexuality in a committed relationship. Particularly there are two words that are often mistranslated in Hebrew Scriptures. *Qadesh* means a male temple prostitute who was regularly involved in ritual sex and the word is regularly mistranslated as "sodomite" or homosexual. The word *to' ebah* means a condemned foreign Pagan religious cult practice, but often is translated as "abomination."

The destruction by fire and brimstone is very real to those who live in a volcanic region, but though God may include the warning of it, the destruction is as a result of the children of Israel being insensitive to God and his desires to be the one glorified and enjoyed by the select people of his choice. Just because of the terror there does not need to be a mention of homosexual individuals, which some modern commentators always imply.

EZEKIEL

In Ezekiel 16:48—50 the Lord says, "As surely as I live, declares the Sovereign Lord, your sister Sodom and her daughters never did what you and your daughters have done. 'Now this was the sin of your sister Sodom; She and her daughters were arrogant, overfed and unconcerned; they did not help the poor and needy. They were haughty and did detestable things before me. Therefore I did away with them as you have seen." We discussed this in the discussion in Genesis, but a further note.

It is hard for us to understand hospitality, but to the Middle Eastern people it was a matter of survival or destruction. Even today there are nations that will go to war in order to provide enough sustenance for their people, and it was the purpose of God that those who came in need would have that need satisfied by his select people regardless of the religious, or lack of religious orientation of those who came.

Dare I suggest that for almost four thousand years the homosexual individuals have suffered from humanity's missed responsibility of taking care of those who are in need, whether, physical, mental or particularly spiritual. But, regardless of their spiritual condition they are persons who need physical sustenance. We are aware that as the Third World Nations exist in a lack of nutrition they do not have the ability to make mental, physical, moral or spiritual decisions.

Possibly the greatest sin that we are committing is the vilification of the homosexual persons to the excluding of our care for those Third World Persons who are in great need. Hundreds of thousands of dollars, possibly millions, have been spent in a campaign concerning the homosexual persons to the exclusion of taking care of the starving who we now can see daily on our television news programs. They are not 'over there' but rather in front of us as we consume junk food and unhealthy beverages.

I question how we can justify spending so much while splitting apart programs that have been successful to bring the Third World Folks up to nutrition par, along with education that will glorify God as well as others in need. Let us emphasize what so many of our mission folk have told us, "Until the world's populations are brought up to par, nutritionally, they cannot make decisions that will openly honor and glorify God. And, an additional world."

Though scripture does not include it, an additional need that must be met by both the heterosexual as well as the homosexual people, should also be considered, that there is a lack of water in the world; that is pure potable water. The lives of people, to say nothing of their agricultural needs, are dependent upon a sufficient supply of water, piped to the centers of population whether large cities or small villages. Global warming with the reduction in size of the glaciers of the continents, which provide rivers of pure water, means that we who have must conserve and consider how to get potable water to those who do not have it. Dare I suggest that there are some keen minds in the homosexual population that have not been used for the good of the world, as they have been forced to continually be on the defensive.

NEW TESTAMENT MUSINGS
ON HOMOSEXUALITY

When I mention two possible homosexual individuals, who have been living together for a period of time, I am often met with the statement, "But they are sinners because of their homosexuality." So in a quiet way I ask for the scripture reference that backs up that statement. Where does Christ say that homosexuality is a particular sin? It certainly was not in the Ten Commandments of the Old Testament. There also is the question of from where the Levitical statement was derived, but it seems impossible to trace that particular statement. Anyway, after asking for the scriptural proof they usually evade the question or go on to something else. When I again ask where the scripture reference is in Christ's ministry they will possibly quote Paul, whose theology we will discuss in a while or they go back to the Levitical statement again.

Therefore I thought it wise to go carefully through the four Gospels that contain the life of Christ to see if there are concerns there that would indicate the truth of their statement. What follows is a careful examination of each of the four gospels. I've studied them several times looking for the evidence of Christ speaking negatively about homosexuality. Again the purpose is to find some illustration of, statement concerning or example that would indicate that Jesus said or thought that the homosexual person is really a specific sinner, uniquely different from other sinners, because of his or her homosexual orientation.

MATTHEW

Matthew was a fair and honest tax collector, who found reality in Jesus Christ and so gave up his tax-collecting profession. Not all tax collectors are crooks. The Roman government had a unique way of collecting taxes. The right to tax was sold to a local person and once it was paid for the Romans backed up the local person. First there was a census, and Jesus was born during one of these times of census, and that determined how many people would be "paid for." The temple tax was different and was paid to the priests for their expenses incurred, whether at time of birth or death or at some other special and sacred time.

Then the tax collector was free to charge anyone, anything, at any time for either themselves or possibly some produce or product that they were carrying along the road. You could be taxed for leaving a village and for entering the village and for many activities within the village that resulted in your making a profit. Have times changed so much?

The tax collector was not a favorite person in the community as he lived with other local folks and fulfilled a need, which was to keep the Romans as far as possible from the local populace. If there were questions, the Romans would always come in to solve the differences and of course they were always there at the time of celebration for the purpose of crowd control. The Romans allowed the practice of the Jewish religion but during such times of gathering they kept a lookout for uprisings. The tax collector probably knew more of the personal lives of villagers than even the local priest, whose main emphasis was at Jerusalem at the time of his special duty.

Matthew's gospel is possibly more Jewish than the other three. He was not an outstanding disciple, he was not a member of the close core of disciples, but then with his background one could really not expect that.

He had found the messiah and was willing to 'go along' until such time as the revelation of Christ's life was needed and then he fulfilled that need by writing the gospel. There may be other emphases in the gospel but suffice it to say that his was the most Jewish of the four gospels.

He might have been the treasurer as he was good with funds, but the treasurer also had to make arrangements in the neighboring villages for food and housing when Christ and his twelve followers, along with others who were camp followers were staying overnight. With Matthew's background he would have had a difficult time convincing folks of his sincerity. But he was called, he answered, and he gives a view of Jesus' life that is a unique and integral picture of Jesus the Messiah.

Matthew has one of the two genealogies and nativity events of Jesus the messiah, with Luke having the other. He covers the early life of Jesus in short order and then goes into detailed coverage of the launching of the Kingdom of God by Jesus. Jesus is shown selecting the disciples, giving the beatitudes and then covering many practical applications of them to the then modern life. Matthew draws attention to Jesus healing and then Jesus sends out the 12 disciples in an early evangelism role.

Jesus' method is to deal with the local Galileans in the villages with both parables and also healing, attesting to the fact that thanks must be given to God for the healings. As the disciples and also camp followers go from village to village they note the consistency of Christ's message. The death of John the Baptist shows the seriousness of the Gospel message with the feeding of 5000 men plus others calling attention to basic truths that the gospel must show itself in practical ways by changing the cultures with which it comes in contact.

The religious rulers become interested and come to hear in person what Jesus is teaching and though he is popular with the local people there is opposition from the Jewish rulers. Jesus continues the healing and teaching but emphasizes the fact that faith is necessary, in him and in his father. The transfiguration links him with the earlier religious fathers and prophets. From the Mount of Transfiguration, he heads south ultimately arriving at Jerusalem. There is much healing and teaching, but also there is a plot by the rulers which leads to the Upper Room fellowship and ultimately the crucifixion and resurrection. Nowhere in Matthew's account is there any mention of homosexuality. The basis for acceptance into the Kingdom, giving God the honor and glory has no sexual consequences and the gospel ends with the great commission to "go and make disciples of all nations." Nowhere in the gospel of Matthew is there the slightest indication that Jesus wants, or even favors the heterosexual individual over and above the homosexual person. When the word "all" is used it includes the homosexual as well as the heterosexual persons.

There are many parts of the gospel that are included in Matthew's account but not in the other three accounts. Therefore it might be wise to briefly examine these to understand Matthew's emphasis. He is the only writer to include the Sermon on the Mount in its entirety. He is the only writer to include the 'ban' about using the Holy Spirit in profanity. He is strong in proclaiming the Kingdom of God and emphasizing the love of Jesus above and beyond the human love of family and associates.

He is also adamant that the leaders of the church should be leaders by example rather than just teachers. The "woes" should be studied possibly in the seminaries of our church.

Jesus' parables of the Kingdom of God include the ten virgins who need to conserve their oil, the giving of the talents to servants while the master is away. But again, there is not the slightest mention of the homosexual person as being in any way different from the heterosexual person in the Christian conscience.

Matthew does include the fact of prayer and instructs us about how to pray. In the 6th chapter, verses 7 to 15 we read, "And when you pray, do not keep on babbling like pagans, for they think that they will be heard because of their many words. Do not be like them, for your Father knows what you need before you ask him. This, then, is how you should pray: 'Our Father in heaven, hallowed be your name, your kingdom come, your will be done on earth as it is in heaven. Give us today our daily bread. Forgive us our debts, as we have also forgiven our debtors. And lead us not into temptation but deliver us from the evil one. For if you forgive men when they sin against you, your heavenly father will also forgive you. But if you do not forgive men their sins, your father will not forgive your sins.'" I would call attention to the phrase, "Your kingdom come, your will be done on earth as it is in heaven."

Later in this study we will find that sex is missing in heaven. There is no mention in the Bible of sex being involved in 'glorifying God and enjoying him', and indeed in any of the words involving the heavenly relationship. Yet, in this model prayer is not Jesus asking us to have an earthly relationship where sex is not that big a deal, as it seems to be not that big a deal in heaven? Following our death, that each of us will experience, there are specific things said about our relationship to Jesus the Christ, but sex, that which constitutes trillions of dollars of concern in the world in everything from advertising to personal daily life, will not be one of them. It does seem that sex is an axle around which all of life is spinning. Scripturally it does not seem that important. Could it be that we are spinning our wheels uselessly? Having spent many years in Alaska I know what it is to spin your wheels and get nowhere but actually digging yourself deeper and deeper in the snow.

MARK

Mark, who is really John Mark, is the author of the second Gospel, probably the gospel that is the most authentic when it comes to chronological sequence. Mark has a unique relationship to Jesus and the disciples. His mother's home was sort of a base of operations for Jesus and the disciples when they were in Jerusalem, so much of what Mark has written could be hearsay but it was probably sitting at the feet of Peter, who notes that Mark is as a son to him. Therefore Mark's gospel, the shortest, has an entry to many of the places where Peter was present to the exclusion of many of the other disciples. Mark's mother's home, if the traditional home is indeed the home mentioned, was built on a corner in Jerusalem with the upper room, a larger banquet style hall being on an additional street. This meant that there were three entrances to the house and if soldiers happened to appear at one entrance the disciples could conveniently leave by some other door and immediately mix with the crowd. Traditionally, the upper room is the place of the last supper.

There was a close relationship of Mark with Peter, even to making a missionary trip. It was on a mission trip with Paul when something went wrong and John Mark returned to Jerusalem. Though Paul felt distant to him at this point these feelings were dispelled later and Paul actually asks Mark to bring Paul's cloak with him to Rome. We can expect Peter's feelings to come through Mark's gospel. Likewise Mark would have knowledge of the good and bad parts of the city of Jerusalem, as it was his home town. It might be here that we discover some relationships concerning the homosexual folk who lived in the city, these relationships being with the secular citizens, not necessarily the Jewish folks, though possibly hidden under a "don't ask - don't tell" situation. There is no such indication. Traditionally Mark is the founder of the church in Alexandria, Egypt, so while not one of the twelve he was instrumental in the expansion of the church early in the century.

Mark's gospel begins with the prophetic announcement of a messiah and immediately goes into the relationship between Jesus and John the Baptist. His gospel has parallels in the other gospels and it is almost as having Peter saying, "This was the time sequence and order that the ministry went," and so chronology is established by Mark along with other comments on the healings, demon possession dispelling and teaching concerning the coming kingdom. He relates the death of John the Baptist and then most of the rest of his book is concerning discourses during the last week of Christ's earthly life. The timing of the various healing acts and also the parables can really be anywhere within Christ's teaching as he repeated such stories to different audiences at various times and different places. Jesus' teachings were valid regardless of where he was geographically, as the villages were similar and it would be difficult to remember such and such a story at such and such a place.

The greatest commandment is given, which is to love the Lord your God and your neighbor as yourself. If that neighbor is a homosexual person then they are also included. This love is an agape style love, a style that for many folks does not exist. Mark gives probably the best explanation of the last earthly days of Jesus in his Gospel, but without a particular specific time sequence. The gospel then moves into the last days of the crucifixion and ends with Christ's resurrection and the ascension. I keep reminding myself that I'm looking for a Biblical justification for the exclusion of any individual or group from full salvation; not just sociological, psychological, philosophical, economic, political or economic. To this point the two preceding gospels do not admit any. Again, there is no direct or even indirect mention of the homosexual individual. There is no indication that Christ, or the early church fathers felt any antagonism toward the homosexual or lesbian person.

LUKE

In the beginning of the Gospel of Luke we find, "Many have undertaken to draw up an account of the things that have been fulfilled among us, just as they were handed down to us by those who from the first were eyewitnesses and servants of the word. Therefore, since I myself have carefully investigated everything from the beginning, it seemed good also to me to write an orderly account for you, most excellent Theophilus, so that you may know the certainty of the things you have been taught." (Luke 1:1-4.)

As are the first two gospels, Luke is also a unique book. The author is probably a doctor or a medical practitioner and he is a gentile, not a Jew. He is writing to another gentile who evidently is a man of means and astute education. Other than that he is not identified. We can surmise that he was involved and a member of the early church, a follower of The Way. As far as the text of the gospel is concerned, Luke never met Jesus the Christ in person. He is also unique because not only did he write a gospel but also a book of the Acts of the Holy Spirit, and the believers. It is very likely he used the other two gospels as sources or used some of the same sources that the other two gospel writers used. That is legitimate for they were men of faith, and indeed here Luke spends some time with Paul who is also a man of faith. These times are identifiable as the text changes from "they" to "we", and back to "they." That favorite definition of FAITH is applicable here, "Forsaking All I Trust Him." Luke trusts the other gospel writers and also Paul, along with the Holy Spirit who is leading all of them.

It is hard to visualize and assimilate but before the presence of Luke along with his writing, the messiah is seen as a Jewish savior for the Jewish world. This was the theological thought of the disciples and only a continual relationship with Jesus changed that. To an extent the disciples had a sense of ownership until Jesus began reaching out, with his words and healings, to the gentiles. In their thinking he was going to get rid of the Romans and the nation would be politically Jewish. It is then difficult to imagine that the gentiles would also be saved, through their faith in the Messiah. That meant that the messiah was not just for the Jewish nation but for all mankind. That possessiveness affects many folks in this day and age, as though they can include or keep out those that they feel should or should not be in the Kingdom. That adds strength to our question about the salvation and equality of the homosexual person, for there are many even today who feel that the homosexual person is not going to experience the spiritual equality of salvation. Ah, but our quest is to give each person an ability to honor and glorify God and enjoy him, forever

And some still believe that homosexual persons should not be in any leadership position. Christ came, though, for every person, regardless of sexual orientation, culture, educational level or political determination, that every person could accept Jesus Christ as savior and glorify God and enjoy him forever. There is not a separate messiah for the homosexual individual. Jesus Christ is that messiah, valid for the gentile or the Jew, the homosexual or heterosexual individual.

It is apparent that Luke is going to use the other two gospels, and possibly other sources that either or both of the other writers consulted, analytically going through them for the substance of his gospel. He is proving the case for the Christian experience and life from a very positive viewpoint and, at the same time for a gentile. He brings the analytical abilities of a doctor to focus on the truth of the life of Christ, statements about him, from him and for all mankind, not just the Jewish but for every individual.

Luke parallels Matthew in telling the birth stories of Jesus and adds richness to the natal epoch. The birth stories are necessary and part of the gentile version of God's coming into the world in the form of a human person. There is an addition to the genealogy of Jesus in that Luke's genealogy goes back to Adam, the beginning of the human race, so that the birth is very important to all mankind, while Matthew's goes only to Abraham, who is the beginning of the Hebrew nation.

The healings, of both physically and mentally sick persons, in this gospel including those of evil spirits, leprosy, and a paralytic, is a natural for Doctor Luke. Where normally a doctor would prescribe and then keep the patient in observation, Luke accepts the healing and does not try to explain why the person was healed, as so many do today with modern sicknesses. The faith of the Roman centurion is observed and the members of a Samaritan village would not accept Jesus and the disciples. This would have been a hot discussion point amongst the disciples, as they talked with one another following the experience, as they were concerned about their messiah being truly theirs. Soon after, Jesus tells the story of the Good Samaritan. Luke's gospel demonstrates the universality of Jesus' teachings.

Additionally, Luke specifically relates the discourse of Jesus concerning the woes of which the disciples were to be careful. They are also applicable to our situation today, and as leaders of the Christian church particularly we should review the woes. I prided myself in my first church for most of the roads were gravel and had pot holes and I knew where they were. If I had disappeared into one of them I might not have been found.

Again this universality is shown in the parable of the Great Banquet, where folks come from the highways, the byways, and all are welcome because Jesus is more than just a local Jewish savior. This universality is also shown in the parable of the Pharisee and the tax collector, and in the attempt of Zacchaeus, a chief tax collector, to see Jesus.

So, though there is much in the gospel about sin and salvation, there is no mention of homosexuality. If it was an issue, and we understand that in secular society it was considered a Roman "thing," there is nothing said in the first three gospels about the subject. Evidently Christ did not see it as an inhibiting sin, though other things are specifically mentioned, that required cleansing before the person came into a saving relationship with God through Jesus Christ his son.

As we have mentioned, Luke is with Paul. This is discovered in (Acts. 20:5) when the pronoun changes from 'them' to 'us'. From this point on we can see Luke accompanying Paul. It must have been a time of much discussion and reflection. Up to this point Luke is relaying what has happened in the life of Peter and then Paul. It was probably at this time that they discussed those of the Roman community who were homosexual and whether they were also included. It was a commonly accepted practice in Roman times for the conqueror to kidnap, or take as slaves young boys and to use them sexually. There are many who today think that it is also a practice approved by our open cultural philosophy. Today it is against the law in every Christian nation where Judeo Christian laws are prevalent. Let us not judge the homosexual person by those who regularly break the law.

Luke is part of the action and he remains such until the action becomes charged between the Sanhedron and the Roman commander over Paul's fate. There is no doubt that Luke and Paul have much to discuss and they evidently have much time to discuss it.

At this point Luke drops out, or rather stands aside while the action continues with Paul and the Roman authorities. Paul declares that he is a Roman citizen so has the right to be tried in Rome which necessitates and guarantees a long trip. When it is determined that Paul will go to Rome, again the action picks up with Luke accompanying him. Paul needed attendants, both for finding sustenance for Paul the prisoner, for the Romans were lax is this aspect of the law, and also because Luke was a doctor and Paul no doubt needed medical help from time to time.

The thorn in the flesh was a continuing problem for Paul. Luke is with Paul, as far as we can tell, until the end of his confinement with the words, (Acts 28:30,) "For two whole years Paul stayed there in his own rented house and welcomed all who came to see him. Boldly and without hindrance he preached the Kingdom of God and taught about the Lord Jesus Christ."

ACTS

It is during these times that the discussions probably covered many different subjects that are not recorded by Luke in the Acts, and no doubt the question of homosexuality came up. We have no record of any discussions at this time but undoubtedly those subjects that Paul wrote about later in his letters to the various churches were discussed with Luke. Both Luke and Paul had a Grecian background and so could intellectually discuss many subjects with total understanding on the part of each.

There is always a question about total understanding when folks of differing cultures get together to discuss a subject. You might think that there is total understanding and then a phrase is used, or a word is used which has different meanings to the two individuals Even translators, who may have been serving for many years, going from one language to another, have difficulty with this. We will mention this again when we review some of the letters written by members of the early church.

No doubt there was discussion about the incident of Peter in Simon the Tanner's home. "I was in the city of Joppa praying, and in a trance I saw a vision. I saw something like a large sheet being let down from heaven by its four corners, and it came down to where I was. I looked into it and saw four-footed animals of the earth, wild beasts, reptiles, and birds of the air.

"Then I heard a voice telling me. 'Get up, Peter, kill and eat.' I replied, 'Surely not, Lord. Nothing impure or unclean has ever entered my mouth.' The voice spoke from heaven a second time, 'Do not call anything impure that God has made clean.' This happened three times and then it was all pulled up to heaven." (Acts 11:5-10) My mind jumps back to creation and God saying that mankind is "good". And, we must remember that the good is for God's sake, not necessarily my or our sake. The scripture that we are and will continue to record is valid for not just the heterosexual folk but also the homosexual folks of the world.

Luke and Paul were no doubt wondering, as they realized that to a Jew they were unclean. But did the question ever arise that possibly the homosexual persons were also unclean persons, but God still wanted them involved in his plan of salvation? There is never any indication that this is true, in the gospel story.

Possibly it is wise at this point to discuss Paul, his life as Saul and the tremendous effect he will have upon the early Christian Church, called The Way, and indeed the effect he has had through the years, through the reformation and upon today's Christian concepts. Paul was born in Tarsus, a Roman province village to a combination of Greek father and Hebrew mother, at least with a Hebrew grandmother.

Paul was a turncoat, and this was and is a difficult fact with which to live, something that folks will claim when a conversion to the Christian faith is involved. He was educated in the Roman community but at the same time educated in the Jewish synagogue. It was there that he rejected any formal future with the Roman authorities and decided to study his faith. The result was a deep desire to serve in Jerusalem in the Sanhedrin, which would be the height of Jewishness, and when we first see him it is in a position where he has gained credence. He must have been in Jerusalem during the crucifixion and also resurrection but he evidently played no part in the events of which we would be concerned.

The story of Stephen is also significant. Stephen was being stoned for being a follower of the Way, the early name for the Christian church and those who were stoning him lay their garments down at the feet of Saul. (Acts 7:54-60.) Stoning was a particularly bloody way of disposing of an individual and if your garments were splashed with the accused's blood they were useless from then on. As reprehensible as it seems to us the Sanhedron was protecting their turf; which included everything spiritual or religious, and according to the Ten Commandments that pretty much involved everything and everybody, and they were acting according to their law. Saul had become so Sanhedronized that he decided to take the battle and persecution of the adherents of The Way, to Damascus. Near Damascus a bright light from heaven flashed around him and he fell to the ground. He heard a voice say to him, "Saul, Saul, why do you persecute me?" Saul answered, "Who are you, Lord?" The voice answered, "I am Jesus of Nazareth whom you are persecuting." (Acts 9:4, 5.) Those who were accompanying Saul evidently returned to Jerusalem and reported the event to the authorities.

Ananias, a believer in Jesus Christ in Damascus was told to seek him out. Acts follows and the conversion was complete. However Paul is a student and hence goes into seclusion for three years again (self-imposed seminary) looking, really studying in depth over the scriptures and realizing that he has been converted by Jesus the master.

It then is mentioned that Paul, now the name he assumes as he is going to work with gentiles, has a thorn in the flesh. It is this author's opinion that the thorn in the flesh is what today we know as trigeminal neuralgia, and it would be wise to understand the medical problem. It begins as a headache located in the upper jaw, and therefore is confused often with tooth problems. As the malady progresses it becomes an intense pain that is experienced once every two or three weeks and then the occurrence is more often.

Ultimately it is continuous and is totally debilitating. (The "thorn in the flesh" is a perfect description of the malady) There are various ways of controlling the pain, but the medical problem is never completely solved. The pain is there but the ultimate treatment is to sever the trigeminal nerve and though the pain continues you cannot feel it. Gamma Knife

Surgery is the present solution with a non-invasive surgery that severs the nerve and others that are close to it. The pain has been likened to birth pangs located between your upper jaw and your brain. It is found mostly in women with about 1 in 20,000 persons having the problem.

Paul probably had the problem, and as time went on it progressed. Therefore the presence of Dr. Luke was very important. Medical doctors, then as now, continually worked to find something that would alleviate the pain. As Luke traveled with Paul he would gather local herbs and use them in mixture, then he would gather new herbs as they progressed to different geographic areas. Many things were probably tried, including the mollusk secretion used by Lydia the seller of purple. Finally the use of acupuncture was found to alleviate the condition for a while, but usually only for a short time and then had to be used again. Luke was probably kept busy keeping Paul in condition to do his evangelistic work. They also probably spent much time in discussing the conditions of the communities and the folks that they encountered.

JOHN

For the basis of this paper I understand that John, the brother of James and the son of Zebedee, is the author of the Gospel of John, the three letters from John and also the Book of Revelation. In (Matthew 20:20), their mother comes to Jesus and asks if he will, "Allow James and John to sit at the right and left hand side of Jesus when he comes into his kingdom."

In (Mark 10:35) the men ask the question, but the answer is the same, "You do not know what you are asking" Jesus says, "Can you drink the cup I drink or be baptized with the baptism I am baptized with?" "We can," they answer and Jesus replies, "You will drink the cup I drink and be baptized with the baptism I am with, but to sit at my right or left is not for me to grant. These places belong to those for whom they have been prepared."

James was the first of the disciples to be martyred for the church. John, his younger brother was one of the first disciples, as both he and Andrew sought out John the Baptist and were his disciples until the return of Jesus from the wilderness. At this time John the Baptizing One pointed to Jesus and both men followed Jesus to be his disciples from that point on. John also was probably the last of the disciples to die.

Most of John's gospel takes place at the latter end of the ministry of Jesus and in the area of Jerusalem. John has been a beloved disciple and uniquely has been part of many of the unique and close relationships that a favored few of the disciples had. There is no reference in either the Gospel, or the letters or the book of Revelation to homosexuals and their lifestyle. There is a remote reference to Gomorrah in the book of Revelation, but it has nothing to do with the homosexual lifestyle.

Outstanding in the gospel and also the letters are the agape love relationships that must be between the believer and Jesus and God and then also between the various believers themselves. They clearly state that our purpose is to glorify God and enjoy him forever, not to criticize and judge others.

Basically there are four words that cover the subject of love in the Greek format. (1) Eros is the sexual or sensual love that our civilization is bombarded with concerning advertising in a capitalistic government. The purchasing of all sorts of goodies is part of eros. (2) Philia is love for family, those who have been given to you as blood relationships. Jesus Christ giving himself on the cross for us is an example of becoming a family through the blood relationship. (3) Storge is the love that we have for the pedestrian, or for the store gazer. This is seen more often in smaller communities because of the huge populations found in the cities. That often comes into play because of the (4) agape relationship which is the giving love that cares not for repayment, but is inspired by God giving his son Jesus the Christ for us. We in turn are inspired to give of what we have and are to serve God and as well as the rest of mankind or civilization, both now and into eternity.

This is often a misunderstood or un-understood concept. If the questioner has been raised in a secular society where selfish love is common, the eros kind is prevalent. However we are not doing good deeds in order to get into heaven, we are entered into heaven because of the Grace, the unmerited goodness that God has for us, and that entry has an entree of Jesus Christ's life, death and resurrection. The distinction between the two concepts is very important as most folk feel that the Christians doing all those good works, giving up all those earthly pleasures and talking only spiritual values are "earning their way" into heaven and that a list of good deeds will be an entry pass for the gates of heaven. No way! Any benevolent thoughts or actions that we have are a result of God's wonderful love for each of us, and for you, the reader.

God loves us, regardless of what we do. He would probably prefer to have us do those good deeds, but in appreciation for all that he has done for us. Roman's 12:9-21 says this well: "Love must be sincere. Hate what is evil; cling to what is good. Be devoted to one another in brotherly love. Honor one another above yourselves. Never be lacking in zeal, but keep your spiritual fervor, serving the Lord. Be joyful in hope, patient in affliction, and faithful in prayer. Share with God's people who are in need. Practice hospitality.

"Bless those who persecute you bless and do not curse. Rejoice with those who rejoice; mourn with those who mourn. Live in harmony with one another. Do not be proud, but be willing to associate with people of low position. Do not be conceited.

"Do not repay anyone evil for evil. Be careful to do what is right in the eyes of everybody. If it is possible, as far as it depends on you, live at peace with everyone. Do not take revenge, my friends, but leave room for God's wrath, for it is written: 'It is mine to avenge: I will repay' says the Lord. On the contrary: 'If your enemy is hungry, feed him; if he is thirsty, give him something to drink. In so doing this, you will heap burning coals on his head.' Do not be overcome by evil, but overcome evil with good." The "burning coals on his heads" was really going way out of your way to help a neighbor at the expense of your time and effort and night's warmth. This advice is for the homosexual as well as the heterosexual individual. There is no distinction of this concept between the two.

One commentator has suggested that if we do the good deeds for an entry pass, then the things that we do selfishly would be against that entry pass, in which case we fail miserably to honor and glorify God and enjoy him forever. A problem that the Christian often has is that it is the best and easiest thing to do the good deeds, and therefore should he or she feel guilty for doing them?

There is no place in the Gospel of John or in the letters of John that would differentiate between the homosexual and the heterosexual person. All persons have come short of the glory of God and each person needs the grace of God to enter into his closer presence. We again encounter the noun and verb forms where God has supplied the nouns and we need to use them as verbs in a way that will honor God and his people (all of whom are our responsibility). For a moment it is fitting to dash back to the Code of Hammurabi where all persons are considered innocent until they show that they are guilty. So here, all people are, or ostensibly are, God's children until they determine intentionally to turn away from his will for their lives.

Early in John's gospel the discussion with Nicodemus brings out the golden passage of the Bible, "For God so loved the world that he gave his one and only son, that whosoever believes in him shall not perish but have eternal life. For God did not send his Son into the world to condemn the world, but to save the world through him." (John 3:16, 17). This statement is not dependent upon a one and only sexual orientation, but is for all who are willing to come out of the darkness into the light of day. John follows, "Everyone who does evil hates the light, and will not come into the light for fear that his deeds will be exposed. But whoever lives by the truth comes into the light, so that it may be seen plainly that what he has done has been done through God." (John 3:20, 21).

Early in his ministry, in discussion with the Samaritan (foreign) woman at the well Jesus makes his first declaration of his messiah-ship when he says to the woman who has had several husbands, "I who speak to you am he, the messiah." (John 4:26) He is the messiah of not only the Jews but of all folks who will believe in him, again with no sexual orientation mentioned. When the chief priests and the Pharisees condemn Jesus the Christ, Nicodemus, (who had gone to Jesus earlier and who was one of their own number) asked, "Does our law condemn anyone without first hearing him to find out what he is doing?" (John7:51) Throughout the Gospel of John, Christ has a continual discourse with the religious leaders of the Jewish nation. Throughout the discourse they attempt to hang him on his words but always he replies in scriptural language and finally retires to where John had been baptizing at the crossing of the Jordan River. The final conflict is between Jesus and the leaders of the nation. This is a constant reminder that we, as Christian leaders need to be utterly careful and sensitive when it comes to leading others in the accomplishment of God's will. Much is expected of us and we bear a huge responsibility to the lay folk whom we lead, but particularly to God.

Rather than a condemnation of the homosexual person, the latter part of the Gospel of John is a condemnation of the Leadership of the Jewish nation. There is a continual use of quoted sayings used to attempt to condemn Jesus with a lingering desire to kill the interference. It is a difficult series of sayings for the leadership of the church, where the church leaders assume more control over the flock than does the shepherd. The latter passages are unfortunately mirrored in many of the theological disputes that swirl back and forth in this day and age. These, attempt to put the spirit of God on "their side", rather than the listening to the spirit of God through the words of Jesus. The struggle briefly ends with Christ on the cross until shortly after the resurrection; then a new hope and faith in Jesus and the church is born.

One does wonder what would have happened had the events not led to the cross. Was there a second possibility? If Jesus had not been crucified at this point would he have continued his peaching mission? Would there have been a stronger emphasis on the gentile, namely the Roman Army? It is difficult to say. He was not interested in political reform, but rather the reform of each individual.

LETTERS OF JOHN

The first, second and third letters of John, found just before the book of Revelation at the end of the New Testament really consist of a love letter to the Dear Children. There is still a great interest in the message of Christ that love is the essential thing. The letter is to the dear children, and the admonition is that they not sin. As each of us is a sinner, the letter is to each of us. In essence it admonishes us to have faith in Jesus Christ and to love all of our neighbors. This means we should love those who might be rejected because the Dear Children have forgotten them, and for this study, that would include the homosexual persons. It should be remembered that love such as is spoken of here is the agape love that binds us all together as Christian folk. Put another way, it means that we should make it possible for all to glorify God and enjoy him together.

REVELATION

We might say that the Book of Revelation is John's crowning glory. He began as an apostle of John the Baptist, and transferred his allegiance to Jesus the Christ. He has gone through his life remembering those very special times, as well as the difficulties that Jesus faced, and he is now at the end of his life. The other disciples have all been replaced with younger folks, who have different views of the Risen Christ. But John, on the Island of Patmos has a revelation. And so John, with his many years of service states:

"The Revelation of Jesus Christ, which God gave him to show his servants, what must soon take place. He made it known by sending his angel to his servant John who testifies to everything he saw – that is, the word of God and the testimony of Jesus Christ. Blessed is the one who reads the words of this prophecy, and blessed are those who hear it and take to heart what is written in it, because the time is near." (Revelation 1:1-3)

He begins with a recitation of things that the churches in the various communities are experiencing and what they should do to correct those various conditions. It is a list that could be well used at the first official meeting of the church boards of the Christian churches even today. As a pastor I sometimes wondered where the congregations that I served would stand in John's estimation. These would be used not as a condemnation, but as an inspiration to inspire the congregation and the members of each church.

What follows is the revelation of the end times when the world does not come into a conclusion but the people of God come into an inclusion into the greater kingdom of God. There have been many interpretations of these chapters, all the way from their being a great dramatic play that John viewed, to a word by word fulfillment of the happenings of the end of the world.

The only reference to anything that might be homosexually involved is in the mention of the word Sodom in the Revelation 11:8. "Their (those who are giving their testimony) bodies will lie in the street of the great city, which is figuratively called Sodom and Egypt, where also their Lord was crucified." But throughout the entire book of the Revelation there is no other differentiation between the heterosexual and the homosexual.

We have read an unpublished manuscript that blames the homosexual persons for most of the destruction in the end times, but there seems to be no relationship expressed in the Revelation that John wrote, though there may be in the apocryphal books. It is not my intent to expound upon those books which are not in the canon.

Pausing momentarily in our discussion of the various books of the Old and New Testaments, it would be good to mention a constant witness as the books were written and now as we read them. This is the presence of the Holy Spirit; that presence of God who guided the earthly authors and who even today as I write and you read, guides our thinking. God's presence is not accepted or followed or even allowed in all of the other sacred writings of the various religious traditions or faiths. There is a reason that the Holy Spirit is not to be included in any negative oath or profanity.

One additional increment is that faith is not necessarily a good thing, but it is dependent upon the object of that faith. To have faith in the wrong thing is often a prelude to destructive thinking and acting. Again, to the Christian FAITH means Forsaking All I Trust Him: referring to God.

In our continuing study we move to Jesus' family and then to the various letters written by Paul, Peter or others. I say others because some authors are questionable. We do not positively know for sure who the authors were. These have been accepted as valid books of scripture, but theologians still question the authorship of some of the written material in God's Word.

JAMES

James is a very interesting person in the New Testament. He knew Jesus in many different ways. First he knew him as a half-brother, probably playing a lot in the small town of Nazareth. It was a hilly community so they went up and down the various streets, knew all the alleys and had a good time together. They also had chores to do each day and they had to get along with their younger sisters, which is often difficult for young boys.

Then James knew Jesus as an older brother. Joseph, their father, died and this meant that Jesus was stipulated very much the older brother determining many things that went on in the home with Mary's help. Jesus was probably in his teens when Joseph passed away and he realized that he had a 'first son' relationship that he had to fulfill. That also meant that James was one step away from being the first son. If Jesus left then James was it.

And Jesus did leave. He had been the mainstay for the family, whether in the home or the synagogue or in the carpenter shop and possibly for the community. Now Jesus was gone on a strange mission; that of convincing folks that he was the messiah. At first the messiah-ship was just a local thought, but as time went on James' role as elder brother assumed a completely different relationship, Jesus was the messiah for mankind. And at times James probably had to defend him when people really questioned whether his older brother was the messiah or not. "Who does he think that he is?" "Well, ask him, watch him."

Then James realized that he himself had to see Jesus as the messiah, and that was not so easy. James had to do something with the family and so he moved them, the brothers and the sisters to Jerusalem. Possibly some of the brothers and sisters stayed in Nazareth, but they were Judeans and at times it was difficult getting along with the Galileans in Nazareth. Then came the time of the cross.

James was at the cross when Jesus looked at Mary and said, "Mary behold your son, and John, behold your mother". (John 19:26.) No doubt James' face flushed at this, "Why involve John in the family responsibilities that he had assumed," but Jesus knew more than James. James needed to be clear, for his new responsibilities would be so great. So it was that he became the head of the Jerusalem congregation of "The Way", the early Christian church. He was involved in the difficult transition from the old Hebrew way of worshipping with sacrifices and legalism to a new way of glorifying God in a more amharitz or common people's way of worship.

And then James also became the mediator between those of the Christian faith who had very staunch concepts and ways of thinking, and each person had seen the Christ from their own point of view. Paul and Peter, both guiding lights of the church seemingly had a difficult time getting along and James had to be that amelioration person in order to allow them to continue with their ministry, so finally James wrote his epistle.

James' job was similar to an automobile service department when you purchase a new or used vehicle. It is wonderful to drive something that isn't going to break down, but the dealer now wants to check it over. Checking it over consists of plugging it into a computer that analyses all its systems, from the pressure in the tires, to exhaust, to engine cooling, to combustion, to transmission, brakes and so on. There are more things than we can comprehend, but they will all be checked and changes made if they are necessary. Even though the car was in perfect condition to start, after a few thousand miles they are still going to check it over.

James is doing the same thing with the young church, and those who have started out in a new faith relationship. As you leaf through the various topics, James is tuning up the life of the individual believer. These topics include, favoritism forbidden, taming the tongue, two kinds of wisdom, giving yourself completely to God, boasting and patience in suffering. Everyone who has made a claim of faith in Jesus Christ as Lord and Savior, and at the time of James's writing there were many, is aware of a new kind of discipline that is needed to fulfill God's "take over" of their lives. Here are a few samples.

"If anyone considers himself religious and yet does not keep a tight rein on his tongue, he deceives himself and his religion is worthless. Religion that God our Father accepts as pure and faultless is this: to look after orphans and widows in their distress and to keep oneself from being polluted by the world." (James I: 26, 27.) "If you really keep the royal law found in Scripture, 'Love your neighbor as yourself' you are doing right." (James 2:8.) "You see that a person is justified by what he does and not by faith alone. In the same way, was not even Rahab the prostitute considered righteous for what she did when she gave lodging to the spies and sent them off in a different direction? As the body without the spirit is dead, so faith without deeds is dead. (James 2:24 – 26.)

But we possibly have one other facet of James' life that bears recognition. He had a nickname, "Camel Knees". Camels kneel on their front knees when mounted or dismounted and James spent so much time in prayer, over the problems of the new young church and also for the ability to get along with emerging theologians who seemed to have a common antagonist, the temple rulers. Spending so much time in prayer on his knees he was known for his long and deep prayers and his calloused knees. It would be good if more of us were willing to spend time on our knees rather than exercising our tongues in condemnation. If you accepted the author's suggestion that you write in the margins of this book you already have a long list of things for which you can pray. We are in perilous times, socially, politically, economically and spiritually. Why don't you pause right now, in the reading of this book, and put your concerns before God. I will do the same in writing. My purpose in writing this book is to honor and glorify God and enjoy his presence.

As a boy and young man James was depending upon Jesus for many of the decisions in his home. Now, after the resurrection, he was depending upon the Christ for the setting of the right direction for the Christian church. It was not going to be a sect of the Jewish faith, there was a totally new relationship with God the Father through Jesus Christ his son.

LETTERS OF PETER

Peter was probably the most outspoken of the disciples. Therefore Jesus found himself answering some questions that only Peter would have thought up during his ministry on the planet earth. Possibly a quote from Peter would set his mood, found in (I Peter 3:8, 9)

"Finally, all of you, live in harmony with one another; be sympathetic, love as brothers, be compassionate and humble. Do not repay evil with evil, or insult with insult, but with blessing, because to this you were called so that you may inherit a blessing." The letters are an encouragement to live and strive to the fullest the Christian life, as we the readers desire to grow the Christian church.

In II Peter 2:6, 7 he mentions the condemned cities of Sodom and Gomorrah as an example of what is going to happen to godless men. I am again reminded that the sin of those homosexual men in Sodom and Gomorrah was not their homosexuality but rather their scorn of God in forcing their sexuality on the angels, "God, you made a mistake in the creation of those people!" Again the question haunts me, do we show that same kind of scorn of and for God? We are to be consistent as God was and is consistent in his creation of a world, presently in our care, but oh so fragile.

Let us hear as the Spirit speaks to us in these passages. "Praise be to the God and Father of our lord Jesus Christ in his great mercy he has given us new birth into a living hope through the resurrection of Jesus Christ from the dead, and into an inheritance that can never perish, spoil or fade--kept in heaven for you, who through faith are shielded by God's power until the coming of the salvation that is ready to be revealed in the last time." (I Peter 1: 3 – 5.) "Live such good lives among the pagans that, though they accuse you of doing wrong, they may see your good deeds and glorify God on the day he visits us." (I Peter 2:12.) "Each one should use whatever gift he has received to serve others, faithfully administering God's grace in its various forms. If anyone speaks, he should do it as one speaking the very words of God. If anyone serves, he should do it with the strength God provides, so that in all things God may be raised through Jesus Christ. To him be the glory and power forever and ever. Amen." (I Peter 4:10, 11.)

"His divine power has given us everything we need for life and godliness through our knowledge of him who called us by his own glory and goodness. Through these he has given us his very great and precious promises, so that through them you may participate in the divine nature and escape the corruption in the world caused by evil desires. For this very reason, make every effort to add to your faith goodness; and to goodness, knowledge; and to knowledge, self-control; and to self-control perseverance; and to perseverance, godliness; and to godliness, brotherly kindness; and to brotherly kindness, love." (II Peter 1:3 – 7) "We did not follow cleverly invented stories, when we told you about the power and coming of our Lord Jesus Christ, but we were eyewitnesses of his majesty. For he received honor and glory from God the Father when the voice came to him from the Majestic Glory, saying, 'This is my Son, whom I love; with him I am well pleased.' We ourselves heard this voice that came from heaven when we were with him on the sacred mountain." (II Peter 1:16 -18) "The Lord is not slow in keeping his promises as some understand slowness. He is patient with you, not wanting anyone to perish, but everyone to come to repentance." (II Peter 3: 9.)

JUDE

Before we discuss the letters of Paul we need to have a brief discussion of Jude. Though he wrote no gospel, he does list himself as a servant of Jesus Christ, and a brother of James, as well as a half-brother of Jesus. The name Jude is also the name Judas and he is listed in other parts of scripture as Christ's brother. I found it interesting to read the entire book (it is short); first, from the homosexual person's viewpoint, and I again read the book from the heterosexual person's viewpoint. Then I read the book from a viewpoint of a homosexual person who feels called to serve Jesus Christ and his church, with an understanding of the homosexual person who has experienced much of the alienation that is firmly established and displayed in many churches and ecclesiastical bodies of many denominations.

One does wonder why Lot stayed in Sodom with his entire family before the incident recorded in scripture. Evidently he got along with the homosexual folks. No trouble developed until the homosexual folk tried to force their sexual orientation onto the angels. Strange how things go well with us until we come to the place where we try to play God and then everything seems to explode, or is it implode?

It is here that our knowledge of the translation of scripture comes into play. Various biblical translations describe the sin as: fornication, going after strange flesh, sexual immorality, perverted sensuality, homosexuality, lust of every kind, immoral acts and unnatural lust. It seems that every translator, being unclear of the meaning of the verse in the original Greek, simply chose the sin of that particular age to be THE sin.

Jude is free with the term "ungodly". I wonder how his thinking would go if he realized that the feelings that the homosexual folk have are those feelings that are natural for persons with their sexual orientation, and according to God they are not ungodly folk. The only things that make them "different" are those things regarding the sexual act. Otherwise they are intelligent, concerned, loving people who are excellent neighbors and, as we look at the list in Galatians 5:22 they are very Godly folk. It is apparent that Christ knew this, hence the lack of condemnation for them. There are many 'serving' groups of workers who appreciate homosexual people due to their work ethic and also the fact that they do not violate sexual mores when they are at work.

It is true that homosexuals may be sinners in many other ways and still need a forgiveness of sin, but they know firsthand what it is like to be crucified without wrongdoing. This gives them a sense of realization of what Christ went through. And of course, we are all sinners, and the homosexual or lesbian person is no greater a sinner because of his or her sexual orientation. Regardless of your inclination or disinclination, the book of Jude is a must and it concludes with the benediction that is used weekly in many congregations, "To him who is able to keep you from falling and to present you before his glorious presence without fault and with great joy – to the only God our savior be glory, majesty, power and authority, through Jesus Christ our Lord, before all ages, now and forever more! Amen." (Jude 25.)

At this point I would remind the reader, and myself, that "the chief end of man is to glorify God and to enjoy him forever." It is also interesting to note that nowhere in the gospels is there any indication that Jesus thought that the homosexual person was any different from a heterosexual person with respect to being a sinner in need of the grace of "God for salvation." If the son of God, as recorded in the four gospels, had no special negative feelings about the homosexual person, then should we?

Possibly at this point it would be wise to mention why the scriptures are being included. When counseling homosexual persons I have been disturbed by their feelings that those who oppose them, often the conservative end of the theological spectrum, use scripture for their own justification. The homosexual persons then feel that scripture is not something that they wish to deal with.

57

My intent in including it is to show that the scripture given, indeed all scripture applies to both the heterosexual and also the homosexual person.

It is also wise, now that we are about to review the letters of Paul, to understand that his letters for the most part were written before there were the written gospels. Though Paul had access to the thinking of Luke, as he spent much time with Luke, he had no access to the gospels of Matthew and Mark, or the sources that they must have used to construct their gospels. The Gospel of John was probably written after Paul's ministry and his death.

At this point let us review again the life, training and experience of Saul or Paul. Saul was born and raised in Tarsus the chief city of Cilicia and it was the residence of the governor of Cilicia. It had excellent schools that Saul attended, but when he showed a proclivity toward legal studies he was sent to Jerusalem and studied under Gamaliel. He was probably conversant in Greek, Latin and Hebrew and was aware of the moral system of Rome, though he had never been there. When the crucifixion and resurrection took place he was probably in the temple studies program. He surfaces in Scripture when Stephen is stoned, as he was the protector of the clothes of those who were doing the stoning. If any blood were to fall on the clothes they would have to be destroyed.

Saul was an A type person and when he realized that there were small groups of these followers of the Way he asked permission to go to Damascus, with a small group to search out the followers. It was near Damascus that he had the conversion vision, was blinded (as though the blinding was blotting out his former life in preparation for a new relationship) and was led to Damascus. His compatriots returned to Jerusalem to report to the authorities, and it was then that Ananias was summoned to bring Saul into the presence of the followers of the Way. His training showed in how "He baffled the Jews living in Damascus by proving that Jesus is the Christ."(Acts 9:22) Paul ended up being a consistent Christian or follower of the Way, angering those he left behind in the Sanhedron.

He had a difficult time because he was a turncoat. Turncoats have multiple difficulties because the groups to which they go always hold them in deep suspicions. They fear the turncoat is really not converted at all, but is merely infiltrating the group. The group from which the turncoat comes continually attempts to discredit the individual. These suspicions often stay with the individual throughout the rest of his or her life, and we find that the person is continually fighting the invisible fact of his former life. We will delve more into this topic as we consider various stands that Paul made concerning his views.

Everyone in the then known world realized the immorality of Rome. Therefore when it comes to understanding Paul's sense of morality, we find that it consists of what he heard about the morality of Rome and what he learned under Gamaliel and what he got in the way of information from those who had known Jesus in the flesh. There are many things that Jesus does not cover as side issues because he was looking for persons to come into direct contact with God, through him, and for each person to glorify God and enjoy him forever. Jesus never talked about slavery, but we know that he would be against it as it disturbed the one to one relationship between the slave person and God.

Jesus never talked about homosexuality because to make a homosexual person 'different,' restricts that person's relationship with God. It was true then and it is true now. Consequently, when we hear Paul talk about moral values they are largely what he learned in Hebrew School. It was still too early in the history of the Christian church to have a formal list of do's and do-not's.

Comparing the moral values of the Hindu religion, Islam, Buddhism, Confucianism, Mormonism and other beliefs is almost impossible, but they all discuss how you treat your neighbor. The fact is we are all neighbors, and Jesus the Christ would have us love our neighbors, in spite of their beliefs.

We must again look at Paul as someone who left the Jewish-only relationship with the Sanhedron and realize that the Jewish leaders would want to discredit Paul. It is no accident that one of the Ten Commandments is, "You shall not give false testimony against your neighbor." In a paperless society your verbal word was very important. Gossips and slanderers were part of those evils with which mankind had to continually deal. It is conceivable that to discredit Paul, who was wandering from town to town with a fellow evangelist, it would be easy to infer that Paul was himself a sexual deviate. Paul could react either by saying that he was not or he could make the case so strong against the homosexual person that people would react, "of course he is not!"

ROMANS

We should discuss verse Romans 1:26. realizing that it is addressed to Rome which was the world's leader in immorality. "Because of this God gave them over to shameful lusts. Even their women exchanged natural relations for unnatural ones. In the same way the men also abandoned natural relations with women and were inflamed with lust for one another. Men committed indecent acts with other men, and received in themselves the due penalty for their perversion." Admittedly there can be immorality in some homosexual relationships, just as there is immorality in some heterosexual relationships. Our actions relate to our faith, in that God wants the total loyalty with each of his created persons. It is not too much to ask of a created person.

I feel that Paul was totally unaware of the present trend of homosexual individuals to form liaisons, usually called partners, with whom they live out their days. Though the sexual act is part of their relationship there is also the family living aspect of their relationship. I find in counseling with them that they often are more concerned with each other than are the participants in some marriage relationships. They do not desire other partners, but wish to remain with their present partners for the rest of their lives.

I believe that if Paul were alive today that he would change his mind concerning many things in light of modern knowledge. Paul had no concept of two homosexual individuals living together in a life-long relationship, which is a present life style possibly more stable that fifty percent plus of the marriages that now are taking place that end in divorce. Paul was and probably would be more concerned with the Grace of God than abiding by the levitical law.

The Holiness Code, Leviticus 17 – 26, was right for God's people in their day but the glory of God's Word is its application and encompassing of the knowledge of the day. It is not anchored in 1000 B.C. or 600 A.D. knowledge. That is because the uniqueness of the Holy Spirit. God is not anchored in the past he is the eternal God; who totally encompasses all time. God does not reject those who come, in faith in Jesus Christ, to him.

In the beginning of his letter to the Romans Paul lists a strong list of those who have incurred the wrath of God. He is familiar with the Roman social society and he waxes eloquent over those who deserve the wrath of God. Beginning with the 29th verse of the first chapter, there is a complete list of those who care not for God or his values. "They have become filled with every kind of wickedness, evil, greed and depravity. They are full of envy, murder, strife, deceit and malice. They are gossips, slanderers, God haters, insolent, arrogant and boastful; they invent ways of doing evil; they disobey their parents, they are senseless, faithless, heartless, and ruthless. Although they know God's righteous decree; that those who do such things deserve death, they not only continue to do these very things but also approve of those who practice them." (Romans 1:29-32) Notice that he includes gossips and slanderers. They rate with the other sins in a sense of equality, and he may have had a real problem with them. In our "instant communication" world it is hard to realize that someone could say something evil about Paul and it would be there and traveling for possibly a year before the wrong was squelched. Like a pillow filled with feathers that has split open with feathers flying in all directions, once the rumors have spread all over, how do you stop all those widely dispersed rumors? Of course to be modern it is putting some falsehood on Face Book and the whole world has access to the lie, though they may not know that it is a lie.

If Paul had ended his letter with this paragraph he would not be welcomed into the Roman society, for most of Roman society the social sisters and brothers, the masters and the slaves, the military or the Emperors and their associates would fall into one or more of the classifications. There were many who would be within the classification of the sinners of Rome.

Paul is not aware of the fact that the decision concerning homosexuality is not a choice of the individual but is due to DNA or other affiliated parts of the created person. In the two thousand years since Paul wrote Romans there has been progress scientifically, in those factors that might affect a person's sexuality, whether heterosexual or homosexual. So far God has not divulged much in the way of knowledge of those factors to the scientists. And God is still creating persons with those attributes and he is still saying "That which I have created is good -- so don't you call evil that which I created, good!" God has chosen those individuals to be the homosexual persons, and it is not their choice.

Also, the homosexual person does not spend his or her entire time dwelling on his or her sexuality. The homosexual person is creative in society, compassionate of neighbors and spends an inordinate time seeking ways to be of service to neighbors and others as we are all taught to be or stated about all people in Romans 2:6,7. "God will give to each person according to what he has done. To those who by persistence in doing good seek glory, honor and immortality, he will give eternal life."

The homosexual couples whom I know usually refer to each other as partners and spend much time discussing things related to their home, their community and their social activities outside of the home. They usually are careful to be an asset to the community and therefore keep their house and their vehicles in good working order. They discuss things that the normal married couple discusses, but possibly because they are homosexual they spend much time planning and carrying out activities that include not only themselves but heterosexual individuals, as well. Normally they maintain close relations with their individual families.

If you read the rest of the book of Romans from the viewpoint of the homosexual or lesbian person, and include yourself among those who are being saved, it is an inspiring book that read daily would well suit your appetite for spiritual sustenance. I recommend that the reader dwell on (Romans 8:37-39)

"No, in all these things we are more than conquerors through him who loved us. For I am convinced that neither death nor life, neither angels nor demons, neither the present nor the future, nor any powers, neither height nor depth nor anything else in all creation, will be able to separate us from the love of God that is in Christ Jesus our Lord."

CORINTHIANS

First Corinthians is a letter to a specific church, or gathering of Christians. Both first and Second Corinthians speak to specific problems that might have existed in the early churches, but at the same time they speak to us in our generation, our age, and there are similar problems in our modern day churches. These, often are problems of our own making. The particular passage that is pertinent to our study is First Corinthians 6:9, 10. "Do you not know that the wicked will not inherit the kingdom of God? Do not be deceived: neither the sexually immoral nor idolaters nor adulterers nor male prostitutes nor homosexual offenders nor thieves nor the greedy nor drunkards nor slanderers nor swindlers will inherit the kingdom of God." Note, they are homosexual 'offenders'. Again, we are reminded of that word *qadesh*, (ritual prostitution) and its often mistranslation.

In the King James Version, homosexuals are called effeminate while in the New International Version they are called homosexual offenders and in the Greek interlinear they are called sodomites. While Paul has been talking of prostitutes one could argue that homosexual persons would be accepted, except for the offenders, those who like those of Sodom were pushing their sexual orientation onto all others. Prostitutes, both female and male, would not be accepted. Again the question rises, is the sin of Sodom that of homosexuality or rather the sin of imposing your own sexual orientation onto everyone you meet, plus a violation of hospitality. Lot had lived in Sodom for quite a while seemingly without problems. Neither the sodomites, nor Lot imposed their orientation on the other group. That is why Lot is willing to offer his daughters because he knows that they will not accept his daughters. If one has ever engaged in conversation with a prostitute one finds they are very normal people except that they often have been forced into the trade, and they do respond to training and habilitation. It is not rehabilitation for that term indicates that they'll become as members of their home, where often the problem first arose.

Today it is possible for many homosexual persons to live in harmony with heterosexual persons if there is no imposition of life style on the other, as enforced by the national law of equality. Live and let live is the rule that permits a spirit of cooperation. Name calling accomplishes nothing at all but disunity. Where there is an imposition then our Christian faith has to work to create and maintain harmony. God is still creating homosexual persons, and if statistics are correct, one of every ten babies born will be a homosexual person. Does God say that is bad? No!

In the fifth chapter Paul says that the Christian fellowship is not to associate with the sexually immoral person, or those that are greedy, idolaters, slanderers, drunkards or swindlers. These are all learned behaviors and the homosexual person is not mentioned. I keep remembering that the purpose of every man and woman is to glorify God and enjoy him forever. This can more easily be done if the homosexual person is not a constant subject of derision.

It seems that since the beginning of time the church has been involved in controversies. These controversies have existed from the time that Terah decided to settle down, though God had called him to move, down through the times of Abraham then to Lot who had his difficulties in Sodom, and on to the settlement of the twelve tribes. These controversies continued on further when John the Baptist decided to turn honest with the religious establishment, and we have listed before the various controversies that have been experienced in the last several years.

GALATIANS

The controversy continued with the ministry of Jesus that was not recognized by the religious rulers of his day, which continued down to the establishment of the church, then known as The Way. The apostle Paul was very important as he broke away, after his conversion and became the head theologian of the church. Within the church there was a strong disagreement between Peter and Paul to which Galatians speaks loudly. The controversy continued on further to the division of the Christian emphasis between Eastern and Western Christianity and then the division between Roman and Protestant leanings, the controversies continue.

In modern times there has been the question of whether people of color could carry the message of a Jewish Messiah and then whether women were capable of carrying that message, until finally today there is the present controversy between the heterosexual and the homosexual person and leadership of a modern congregation, which is composed of heterosexual and homosexual folk, the controversies seem to continue.

There are some who feel that these controversies are necessary to "cleanse" the spirit of the Church. The church has endured the deviousness, the suspicion, anger and the mean spirit but how wonderful when the heads of the church, led by the Holy Spirit, can once again reconcile their differences realizing that to be united in Christ far outweighs any spite the splits engender.

Times change, cultures change, political power bases change, geography and science change but through all the controversies is the consistent emphasis in the Bible that God desires every individual to come to him to glorify God and enjoy him. There is a love that God has shown for mankind, every individual of mankind, and in responding to that love the faith of a person becomes very lively. But that faith is anchored in God's Word and through all the controversies persons have struggled to find God's Will through all the changes. Let's go back to Galatians, for there the Holy Spirit lays out a basis for judgment concerning the controversies.

Galatians speaks first of the authority of Paul, establishing it through a call of God. Then the controversy between Paul and Peter erupts, mainly over circumcision. Some felt that to become a follower of Jesus one had to be circumcised first, become a Jew and then they would be able to accept Christ as savior. Ultimately, did one have to be a Jew before he or she became a Christian? This also inferred that Christianity was a little side cult of the main basic Jewish faith. Christians claimed the Jewish tradition as their own and Jesus was of the Jewish tradition. Circumcision was a sign of Jewishness, something that could not be reversed.

Paul intensifies the discussion by mentioning that the Christian has a spiritual circumcision, a removal of the old coating of sin with the acceptance of the new savior, Jesus the Christ. Which is more important, the faith or the observance of the law? And the arguments went and go heavily toward faith. That faith must be anchored in the life, death and resurrection of Jesus the Christ.

In the closing section of Galatians, the fifth Chapter beginning with the 19th verse, we read, "The acts of the sinful nature are obvious: sexual immorality, impurity, and debauchery, idolatry; and witchcraft; hatred, discord, jealous, fits of rage, selfish ambition, dissentious factions and envy; drunkenness, orgies, and the like. I warn you, as I did before, that those who live like this will not inherit the Kingdom of God." Note that these sins are not listed in ascending or descending order. No one sin, is more sinful than any other sin, nor is any sin defined in detail so that legally you could operate within the sin while showing a crust of Christian concern to the outside world.

Earlier Paul acknowledged that to commit one sin is to be guilty of many of the others. He says it much more judiciously, but that is the point. Though a current branch of Christianity does qualify the various sins in venal and menial, such does not take place here. Nor does this qualification take into account the fact that homosexual orientation determines that by nature it is correct when following its orientation, though this may not be understood by the heterosexual multitude.

I must confess that when listing those various sins I have instantly, and with no malice aforethought, thought of how they would stack up against the modern culture where many of them are regularly accepted not only on the street and in our homes, but also through the modern media outlets. Should we say that it is the dumbing down of our modern Christian culture, of which we speak so often? It is a sad commentary on our times that have wandered so far from the Christian faith that we quietly brag about in our modern American culture.

But Paul is not finished. He continues in Galatians 5:22. This is a very pregnant chapter indeed, but not of the nine month variety, "But the fruit of the spirit is love, joy, peace, patience, kindness, goodness, faithfulness, gentleness and self-control. Against such things there is no law. Those who belong to Christ Jesus have crucified the sinful nature with its passions and desires. Since we live by the spirit, let us keep in step with the Spirit. Let us not become conceited, provoking and envying each other." (Maybe we should add these three to the preceding list of sins?)

But the question remains, is it necessary to continually speak of belonging to the Spirit or is it better to just act without continually broadcasting that you are acting with the Holy Spirit in mind? I find many of my homosexual friends are acting in the presence of the spirit but do not articulate that what they are doing is a fruit of the spirit. Paul answers the question in Galatians 6:7. "Do not be deceived: God cannot be mocked. A man reaps what he sows. The one who sows to please his sinful nature, from that nature will reap destruction; the one who sows to please the Spirit, from the Spirit will reap eternal life."

Again it is wise to remember that our purpose on earth or beyond is to glorify God and enjoy him forever. That which we say, do, think, and reveal in our lives is this purpose every person has that as his or her main object. It is not our purpose to draw lines around what we view as the truth and keep out those who refuse to agree with us. Rather we are to be in selfless service and include all whom we can in the fellowship, for such action honors God who created, creates and will create all things and persons. God has given us his son, and it is up to us to verbalize, whether with words or actions, the person of Jesus Christ.

EPHESIANS

Ephesians is an interesting letter. There are many scholars who feel that Ephesus was Paul's home church, and that there was the residence of his wife, if he had one.

There is another group of scholars who feel that this was Paul's supreme letter, that it was the letter that positively circulated through the various churches in Asia, that the early manuscript of this letter did not contain a destination but that the letter was passed around from church to church. It was never owned by one congregation but was possibly copied and then sent on to other followers of the Way.

Therefore I would like to treat this as a letter to us, today. And so I'd suggest that we gather to listen to what the Holy Spirit has to say through Paul in this letter. Rather than just copying the letter I'll select various passages but it will be the Holy Spirit speaking through Paul to us.

Gathered will be possible members of the church including new converts, long time members, clergy and lay folk, children old enough to understand, middle aged persons beginning to look at retirement and those who are now retired. Those gathered include Christians, and Jews, Moslem, Buddhist and Hindu as well as totally non-believers, and wanna-bee's, persons who would love to be Christian but because of political conditions they find it impossible. Those gathered include prostitutes, pimps and the johns, (customers of prostitutes). They will include heterosexual and homosexual and transvestite folks, include women and all men, whether they are including themselves or trying to exclude themselves.

Each of us has been created by God, whether they think so or not and we are treading the earth that he created. The listeners will include

Americans, Canadians and all South Americans. Included will be Asiatics, Africans and Middle Easterners, Europeans and folks from every continent on the planet earth. Included will be those who are incarcerated, some for the rest of their lives, but then we are all incarcerated on the planet for the rest of our lives, and that is good. There will be 7 billion + of us, but the Holy Spirit is speaking to each of us individually, to Ken and Betty Smith, to each of our kids and all of the kids who are reachable through cell phone, internet, or personal visit. The listeners will include all cultures, and language groups, no one will be excluded for each of us occupies a particular place on the planet earth yes and we will also include those in the space station for they are earthlings. Each one of us is special to God, he created us and so this message is for each one.

"For it is by grace that you have been saved, through faith—and this not from yourselves, it is the gift of God—not by works, so that no one can boast. For we are God's workmanship, created in Christ Jesus to do good works, which God prepared in advance for us to do." (Ephesians 2:8-10.)

"Consequently you are no longer foreigners and aliens, but fellow citizens with God's people and members of God's household, built on the foundation of the apostles and prophets, with Christ Jesus himself as the chief cornerstone. In him the whole building is joined together and rises to become a holy temple in the Lord. And in him you, too are being built together to become a dwelling in which God lives by his Spirit." (Ephesians 2:19-22).

"For this reason I kneel before the Father, from whom his whole family in heaven and on earth derives its name. I pray that out of his glorious riches he may strengthen you with power through his Spirit in your inner being, so that Christ may dwell in your hearts through faith. And I pray that you, being rooted and established in love, may have power, together with all the saints to grasp how wide and long and high and deep is the love of Christ, and to know his love that surpasses knowledge—that you may be filled to the measure of all the fullness of God." (Ephesians 3:14-19.)

"Do not let any unwholesome talk come out of your mouths, but only what is helpful for building others up according to their needs, that it may benefit those who listen. And do not grieve the Holy Spirit of God with whom you were sealed for the day of redemption. Get rid of all bitterness, rage and anger, brawling and slander, along with every form of malice. Be kind and compassionate to one another, forgiving each other, just as in Christ God forgave you." (Ephesians 4:29-32.)

"Therefore do not be foolish, but understand what the Lord's will is. Do not get drunk on wine, which leads to debauchery. Instead, be filled with the Spirit. Speak to one another with psalms, hymns and spiritual songs. Sing and make music in your heart to the Lord, always giving thanks to God the Father for everything in the name of our Lord Jesus Christ. Submit to one another out of reverence for Christ." (Ephesians 5:17-21.)

"Finally, be strong in the Lord and in his mighty power. Put on the full armor of God so that you can take your stand against the devil's schemes. For our struggle is not against flesh and blood, but against the rulers, against the authorities, against the powers of this dark world and against the spiritual forces of evil in the heavenly realms. Therefore put on the full armor of God, so that when the day of evil comes, you may be able to stand your ground, and after you have done everything to stand. Stand firm, then with the belt of truth buckled around your waist, with the breastplate of righteousness in place, and with your feet fitted with the readiness that comes from the gospel of peace. In addition to all this, take up the shield of faith, with which you can extinguish all the flaming arrows of the evil one. Take the helmet of salvation and the sword of the Spirit, which is the word of God. And pray in the Spirit on all occasions with all kinds of prayers and requests. With this in mind, be alert and always keep on praying for all the saints. Peace to all the brothers, and love with faith from God the Father and the Lord Jesus Christ with an undying love." (Ephesians 6:10-18, 23, 24.)

PHILIPPIANS

In the letter to the church at Philippi, Paul stresses the humility of Jesus Christ. Though Paul has all the membership conditions for the Jewish faith, it is the humility of Jesus Christ that moves Paul to one of the greatest statements found in scripture, (Philippians 2:5-11.) "Your attitude should be the same as that of Christ Jesus: Who, being in very nature God, did not consider it equality with God something to be grasped, but made himself nothing, taking the very nature of a servant, being made in human likeness. And being found in appearance as a man, he humbled himself and became obedient to death--even death on a cross! Therefore God exalted him to the highest place and gave him the name that is above every name, that in the name of Jesus every knee should bow, in heaven and on earth and under the earth; and every tongue confess that Jesus Christ is Lord, to the glory of God the Father."

"Every knee", doesn't mean just heterosexual folks, or Americans, or any special group. It means all people who come with the same humility that Paul showed, and this includes our homosexual and lesbian folk. There is no distinction made here as to sexual orientation. Those who are heterosexual have room in their relationship for Jesus the Christ and those who are of homosexual relationship have that same room. And they are under the same injunction as Paul, found in the (Philippians 4:8, 9,) "Finally, brothers, whatever is true, whatever is noble, whatever is right, whatever is pure, whatever is lovely, whatever is admirable—if anything is excellent or praiseworthy—think about such things. Whatever you have learned or received or heard from me or seen in me—put it into practice. And the God of peace will be with you."

I have been continually impressed by the cleanliness, the order and the beauty of what seems to be the result of homosexual creativity and upkeep. I remember living in the San Francisco area where homosexual folks were invited and urged to move into various communities in the city because they were such a positive addition to the communities. They immediately began improving their own homes and were active in civic groups in the improvement of the community.

In Paul's letter to the Philippians one senses his frustration at being kept on hold, in his house arrest in Rome, when he wants to be out and about. So he emphasizes many seemingly imperative verbs. "And this is my prayer; that your love may abound more and more in knowledge and depth of insight." (Philippians1:9.) "Whatever happens, conduct yourselves in a manner worthy of the gospel of Christ." (Philippians1:27a.) "If you have any encouragement from being united with Christ, if any comfort with his love then make my joy complete by being like-minded, having the same love being one in spirit and purpose. Do nothing out of selfish ambition or vain conceit, but in humility consider others better than your selves." (Philippians 2:1-3.)

"Continue to work out your salvation with fear and trembling, for it is God who works in you to will and to act according to his good purpose." (Philippians 2:12-13.) "Finally, my brothers, rejoice in the Lord." (Philippians 3:1.) "Join with others in following my example, brothers and take note of those who live according to the pattern we gave you." (Philippians 3:17.) "Finally, brothers, whatever is true, whatever is noble, whatever is right, whatever is pure, whatever is lovely, whatever is admirable—if anything is excellent or praiseworthy—think about such things. Whatever you have learned, or received or heard from me or seen in me—put it into practice. And the God of peace will be with you." (Philippians 4:8,9.) He concludes this epistle with, "To our God and Father be glory forever and ever. Amen." Philippians 4:20. "Greet all the saints in Christ Jesus. The grace of the Lord Jesus be with your spirit. Amen." (Philippians 4:21, 23.)

Regardless of from what orientation you come, scripture speaks to you as a person. In a world of turmoil with everyone trying to be somewhat better than each of us really is, we need to remember that in a few short years we will be part of the historical past. That which we did probably will be forgotten, books that we wrote out of print, and no longer available on iPads, financial empires turned to dust, but the Holy Spirit of God will continue in those who have been impressed with our very quiet but profound witness. And, who knows? Possibly the world will finally come to realize that the God of scripture, the God of all creation, of grace has prevailed. The horror packages of which we have heard will have come under the power of the Holy Spirit and the horror will not have to take place for the love of God, for all of his creation will prevail. Injected into every prayer that we pray should be a prayer for those who violently reject the Christian faith, and when is the last time that you prayed for the opposition?

THESSSALONIANS

The letter to the church of the Thessalonians probably was written by a committee. Paul was the primary author, and he was authoritative. He signed the letter with his own signature, but he realized that his writing had been rather sharp and it would be wise to mellow out, to show some of that love that he talks about. Probably Silas, his partner in mission and Timothy, who was probably the *amanuensis*, (that is the Greek word for secretary) were probably the co-authors, giving their suggestions about the salient points as well as their encouragement. Paul realized that his letters were read by many different groups so what he says to one would be heard by many others as more and more copies of the letters were sent out to new groups of believers. The second letter to the Thessalonians deals with probable problems in the church including the idleness of those who are busybodies but not busy bodies.

The conclusion of the first letter could well express the salutation Paul, Silas and Timothy give, "Now we ask you brothers, to respect those who work hard among you, who are over you in the Lord and who admonish you. Hold them in the highest regards in love because of their work. Live in peace with each other. And we urge you brothers, warn those who are idle, encourage the timid, help the weak, be patient with everyone. Make sure that no one pays back wrong for wrong, but always try to be kind to each other and to everyone else. Be joyful always, pray continually; give thanks in all circumstances, for this is God's will for you in Christ Jesus. Do not put out the Spirit's fire; do not treat prophecies with contempt. Test everything. Hold on to the good, avoid every kind of evil." (I Thessalonians 5:12-22.)

There is a positive spirit in this passage that just feels good. It is true that there are many evil things in the world but our admonition is not to spend all our time fighting others, arguing whether this or that denomination, or theological stand is more correct than any other, but to rather in all our activities exude the beauty and love of Christ on and to all we meet. The world is in such an admitted mess, with constant upheaval in economics, morals, political ends and geographical considerations. We feel we should just look at that last paragraph, from scripture, and do it!

The subject of sexual immorality is possibly touched upon (I First Thessalonians 4: 3 to 8) "It is God's will that you should be sanctified: that you should avoid sexual immorality (which was so prevalent in the middle eastern communities but does not include homosexual relations with a same--partner relationship) that each of you should learn to control his own body in a way that is holy and honorable, not in passionate lust like the heathen, who do not know God: and that in this matter no one should wrong his brother or take advantage of him. The Lord will punish men for all such sins, as we have already told you and warned you. For God did not call us to be impure, but to live a holy life. Therefore he who rejects this instruction does not reject man but God, who gives you his Holy Spirit." And what does this say to the homosexual couple who have been true to each other for years?

Timothy's report of p-mail, which is personal mail, would be welcome, but there were still small groups that held differing views about all sorts of things and these are the concern of Paul, who is not yet free to visit the various churches. Paul longs to see the folks in Thessalonica. It is true that with the busyness of his time in Rome, and the uncertainty of his future he needs good news of Christ's church's growth in various places that he has visited. If it were not for the conditions of his ministry throughout the early church, true the letter would almost seem egotistical, but in fact Paul was living his faith and therefore could honestly say, "Look at me, see what I've said and what I've done."

Immorality is a reality in the homosexual community as well as in the heterosexual community. I have found, though, that when a homosexual couple find the perfect partner, that there is a staunch dedication to the other member of the couple. The behavior of the heterosexual folks in the introduction could also have been a problem in the homosexual community also. We'll discuss more on immorality later in our thinking.

COLOSSIANS

The letter to the church at Colossi is similar to other letters of Paul, but he lists the rules for holy living, acknowledging that once the readers lived in those earthly rules, "But now you must rid yourself of anger, malice, slander, and filthy language from your lips." (Colossians 3:8.)

The gist of Colossians is found in Colossians 3:11 to 17. "Here there is no Greek or Jew, circumcised or uncircumcised, barbarian, Scythian, slave or free, but Christ is all and is in all. Therefore, as God's chosen people, holy and dearly loved, clothe yourselves with compassion, kindness, humility, gentleness and patience. Bear with each other and forgive whatever grievances you may have against one another. Forgive as the Lord forgave you. And over all these virtues put on love which binds them all together in perfect unity. Let the peace of Christ rule in your hearts, since as members of one body you were called to peace. And be thankful. Let the word of Christ dwell in you richly as you teach and admonish one another with all wisdom, and as you sing psalms, hymns and spiritual songs with gratitude in your hearts to God. And whatever you do, whether in word or deed, do it all in the name of the Lord Jesus, giving thanks to God the Father through him." Our purpose is to honor and glorify God and enjoy him, and the lesbian, homosexual or heterosexual person is totally involved.

There is a unity in the Christian fellowship and this is emphasized in Colossians 3:10, 11. "You have put on the new self, which is being renewed in knowledge in the image of its creator. Here there is no Greek or Jew, circumcised or uncircumcised, barbarian, Scythian, slave or free, (I believe that were Paul alive today and asked that he would include homosexual or heterosexual, author's addition) but Christ is all and is in all." Paul concludes by sending greetings to his friends in the congregation.

The controversy of Paul's day, mentioned above, was whether or not you had to be circumcised before entry into the Christian faith. It crept into every letter, and Paul answers the questions again by mentioning that there is a spiritual circumcision, which is ridding oneself of sins that would get in the way of glorifying God so that one may completely honor and glorify God and also enjoy the process. He writes often of singing spiritual songs and hymns that tended to unite the congregations of his day.

This presents a problem in this day and age as we transition from Psalms (in my Scotch Covenanter background) and hymns into the praise teams and a more modern, though at times transitory form of gospel song. Fortunate are those congregations of Christian Churches that blend the two in one glorious hymn sing with praise song interludes.

TIMOTHY

Timothy is the true son in the faith. In a sense, Timothy is the 'next' generation and therefore Paul is greatly concerned about his ministry. I accept the fact that many are called to minister in the life of the faith and the church, but I also theologically and practically believe that the person called to service is used by God's Holy Spirit. We really are vehicles used by God to do his will. In some cases it is true the holiness rubs off on the vehicle and in some cases it does not, but again the purpose of the vehicle, or the minister, missionary or lay Christian is to honor and glorify God and enjoy doing so. It should be and is fun being in Christian service. A lot of questions that might have been raised are already answered because of the direction that the vehicle is going.

I'm reminded of Yogi Berra's statement that says, "When you come to a 'Y' in the road, take it." It sounds impossible in practicality but in the practicality of Christian ministry, whether ministerial or lay oriented it is often possible to do just that. The road accepts different or divergent viewpoints, but if they are covered by agape love this is not theory, it is practicality the Y is not only possible but actual.

One of the controversies in the long history of the Christian church has been the place of women in the church. In reading Paul's thoughts concerning women we may gain a further insight into the questions of homosexuality. In his first letter to Timothy, we have to remember the environment in which it was written. Rome, for all its good points, still treated women as chattel. Most of the rulers had not only one wife but several concubines, so Paul's attempt was to have a special role for women in the church. And of course there were temples in all of the cities and most of the towns that used women as priests and also as temple prostitutes. I do wonder what he would have thought of the present day with many women very successfully active in the leadership of the church, as well as in collegiate and seminary teaching. Some are seminary presidents. His discourse on widows is interesting and gives credence to the fact that possibly he should have had a women edit some of his thinking, but again we should be aware of the culture of his day.

For those who might have strong feelings about this book, <u>Homosexual Theology</u>, I would suggest that (Timothy 5:1) contains good words, "Do not rebuke an older man harshly, but exhort him as if he were your father. Treat younger men as brothers."

To continue with Paul's feelings about elders, his thoughts are continued in I Timothy 5:17, 18. "The elders who direct the affairs of the church well, are worthy of double honor: especially those whose work is preaching and teaching." For the Scripture says, 'Do not muzzle the ox while it is treading out the grain,' and 'The worker deserves his wages.'" We have seen these positive actions in the lives of several homosexual persons who have been active in the leadership life of the church, and have experienced the comradery as the heterosexual and homosexual elders work together for the good of all the church.

Paul's second letter to Timothy is rather personal. It says "To Timothy, my dear son". (2 Timothy 2:2.) If you read behind the lines you sense a frustration when life seems to close in on you. Paul honestly mentions many who have left the faith and who question his own faith. In a sense, it is a warning when Timothy is actively involved in his own mission. It is a shame when folks have to be involved in a lack of faith, when God is so good. The book of Timothy contains what has become a guiding passage for the author in his ministry that has included all three forms, Hierarchial, Presbyterian and Congregational of church relationship.

II Timothy 2:14–16. Says, "Keep reminding them of these things. Warn them before God against quarreling about words; it is of no value, and only ruins those who listen. Do your best to present yourself to God as one approved, a workman who does not need to be ashamed and who correctly handles the word of truth. Avoid godless chatter, because those who indulge in it will become more and more ungodly." Having spent hundreds of hours in committee meetings where we argued about words, what they said and what they meant, this passage has great meaning to me.

One of the things that I encountered in my multi-cultural congregations was that words were often a handicap, not an asset to a problem. I would say something, but what I said and what they heard might be completely different. I also found that there were many Hawaiian and Japanese words that carried much more meaning than I could amass in possibly a sentence or two.

We have spent hours in committee meetings, both church and also local and state government wrangling over words that basically said the same thing, but which seemed to get in the way of positive thoughts and issues. The issues became personal problems rather than concept concerns. Strangely we have found that humor was the knife that would separate the various sides

In his final charge in the first letter, following the 'love of money', paragraphs Paul sums up the charge to Timothy and to possibly all who minister in the church, "But you, man of God, (or woman) flee from all this and pursue righteousness, godliness, faith, love, endurance and gentleness. Fight the good fight of the faith. Take hold of the eternal life to which you were called when you made your good confession in the presence of many witnesses. In the sight of God, who gives life to everything, and of Christ Jesus, who while testifying before Pontius Pilate made the good confession, I charge you to keep this command without spot or blame, until the appearing of our Lord Jesus Christ, which God will bring about in his own time—God the blessed and only Ruler, the King of kings and Lord of lords, who alone is immortal and who lives in unapproachable light, whom no one has seen or can see. To him be honor and might forever. Amen. (I Timothy 6:11–16.)

The homosexual person who also makes a confession of faith and is a leader in the church is equal to accepting this charge. In light of the fact that we are going to spend eternity together it is honest to be together now in ministry.

TITUS

The book of Titus is known as the Apostles letter, or sometimes gospel. It is written with eternal life in view and that the servant, *dulos*, really slave of God has certain responsibilities, and these are listed in Titus. Titus was on Crete, not known as a holy place, so the qualifications that Paul lists seem extreme, but are sincere. These qualifications are, "For the grace of God that brings salvation has appeared to all men. It teaches us to say 'No' to ungodliness and worldly passions, and to live self-controlled, upright and godly lives in this present age, while we wait for the blessed hope –-the glorious appearing of our great God and Savior, Jesus Christ, who gave himself for us to redeem us from all wickedness and to purify for himself a people that are his very own, eager to do what is good. These, then, are the things you should teach. Encourage and rebuke with all authority. Do not let anyone despise you. " (Titus 2:11-15.)

Titus takes less than five minutes to read, but possibly this short book should be read monthly by every pastor of every Christian congregation. Then we could, "But avoid foolish controversies and genealogies and arguments and quarrels about the law, because these are unprofitable and useless. Warn a divisive person once, and then warn him a second time. After that, have nothing to do with him. You may be sure that such a man is warped and sinful; he is self-condemned." (Titus3:9-11.)

Particularly noted is the fact that you should not take part in the controversies, arguments and quarrels about the law. Often when the grace of God is forgotten the leaders spend their time arguing about the major and minor shades of the law. Such is deleterious to the spiritual health of the followers of Jesus Christ. The gospel ends with the simple but profound phrase, "Grace be with you all." (Titus 3:15)

PHILEMON

Philemon is a letter from Paul and Timothy to Philemon, Philemon's wife and the church that meets in his home. The story is that Onesimus, a slave of Philemon, has run away and has found Paul. Under Paul's ministry Onesimus is converted to The Way. He then returns with the letter to Philemon, still as a slave but under the recommendation of Paul that he be received as a brother. We presume that Onesimus was welcomed home and this did happen as the letter is witnessed by Epaphras, Mark, (John Mark), Aristarchus, Demas and Luke (the doctor), Paul's fellow workers. In background it was a standard practice for the Roman soldiers or gentlemen to keep male slaves to be used as homosexual servants. Very often the slave was seen this way whether or not he was so used. In Philemon's case it was not so, therefore Paul urges him to receive Onesimus as a brother.

Unfortunately it reminds me of a sadder story that did happen. A young man of my acquaintance realized that he was homosexual and fought with that fact for many months. Finally he went to his parents and explained that fact to them. Unlike the story of Onesimus, the young man was not welcomed. They immediately removed him from the family, disinherited him and cut off any physical or spiritual support that he might receive and in essence locked the door to the family and threw the key away. Tragically the young man ended his own life and it ultimately resulted in the sad and angry death of both parents, and the further hurt in that the pastor of their church totally supported them in their decision.

HEBREWS

We conclude our speedy walk through the Bible with the book of Hebrews. This book is a mystery because just who the author was is unknown. There are many candidates ranging from the early missionaries to later theologians. The author was very familiar with the ritual worship of the temple and at the same time uses a form of Greek that is excellent, almost too perfect for someone out of or on the edge of the realm of Greek thought and discourse.

I have always thought of the book of Hebrews as being the transition letter that ties the revelations of God in the ritualistic worship of the Old Testament to the New Testament expression of worship. Evolution is supposedly a bad word, but really the knowledge of God's will and the worshipful expression of adoration to God do evolve from early stories of God's presence, to the fathers of the faith, Abraham, Isaac, Jacob (and they are listed in this book) to the temple worship. Ultimately through this volume of Hebrews, New Testament worship evolves and an expression of Faith in Jesus Christ as Lord and Savior of the Body of Christ is an integral part of worship in the church of first the Way and then the Christian Church.

The transfer of the blood of cleansing in the Old Testament has close ties with the blood that Jesus shed in our salvation process. The passing through the curtain that separated the Holy of Holies from the Holy Place in the temple, the main worship area for the Hebrews, is made accessible through Jesus Christ. Chapter 11 is particularly insightful as we step into the list of those who 'through faith'--- we continue the witness to Jesus Christ by faith in him, and we must be careful that faith that is not in Jesus Christ can be false faith. This true faith is open to all people, of all ages, conditions, cultures, and sexual orientations. The following is a taste of the book of Hebrews.

"In the past God spoke to our forefathers through the prophets at many times and in various ways, but in these last days he has spoken to us by his Son whom he appointed heir of all things, and through whom he made the universe. The Son is the radiance of God's glory and the exact representation of his being, sustaining all things, by his powerful word. After he had provided purification for sins, he sat down at the right hand of the Majesty in heaven. So he became as much superior to the angel as the name he has inherited is superior to theirs. For to which of the angels did God ever say, 'You are my Son; today I have become your father'? Or again, 'I will be his Father, and he will be my son'?" (Hebrews 1:1-5.)

"Therefore, since we are surrounded by such a great cloud of witnesses, let us throw off everything that hinders and the sin that so easily entangles, and let us run with perseverance the race marked out for us. Let us fix our eyes on Jesus, the author and perfecter of our faith, who for the joy set before him endured the cross, scorning its shame, and sat down at the right hand of the throne of God. Consider him who endured such opposition from sinful men, so that you will not grow weary and lose heart." (Hebrews12:1-3.)

"Make every effort to live in peace with all men and to be holy; without holiness no one will see the Lord. See to it that no one misses the grace of God and that no bitter root grows up to cause trouble and defile many. See that no one is sexually immoral, or is godless like Esau, who for a single meal sold his inheritance rights as the oldest son. Afterward, as you know, when he wanted to inherit this blessing, he was rejected. He could bring about no change of mind though he sought the blessing with tears." (Hebrews 12:14-17.)

"Keep on loving each other as brothers. Do not forget to entertain strangers, for by so doing some people have entertained angels without knowing it. Remember those in prison as if you were their fellow prisoners, and those who are mistreated as if you yourselves were suffering. Marriage should be honored by all, and the marriage bed kept pure, for God will judge the adulterer and all the sexually immoral. Keep your lives free from the love of money and be content with what you have, because God has said,

'Never will I leave you; never will I forsake you.' So we say with confidence, 'The Lord is my helper; I will not be afraid. What can man do to me?' Remember your leaders, who spoke the word of God to you. Consider the outcome of their way of life and imitate their faith. Jesus Christ is the same yesterday and today and forever." (Hebrews 13:1-8.) Again hospitality is an important ingredient for the Christian life.

There is one more area that I alluded to in an earlier section, and that is the place of sexuality in heaven. I remember that our chief end (purpose) is to glorify God and enjoy him forever. God did not make us for ourselves but for fellowship with him.

THE FELLOWSHIP

There is a fellowship of those who follow Jesus the Christ. Yes, there are many different denominations, some that are very liberal and some that are very conservative, and those two distinctions can be broken down in theology, politics, social action, worship styles and just about every different emphasis. That fellowship can easily begin with the prayer, "Now I lay me down to sleep. I pray the Lord my soul to keep. If I should die before I wake I pray the Lord my soul to take." "Gentle Jesus meek and mild, have pity on me a little child."

Yes, the early relationship with God is through prayers that may be memorized, but never the less are very real. Fortunately children are naïve and honest enough to really want to know about God and their relationship with him. As children age so should their relationship with God.

The Lord's Prayer is the fulfillment of relationship with God. To analyze it and follow the various themes that it announces helps a person relate to

God. Often our prayer is just a request, or a frantic last minute calling on God to alleviate some difficult situation.

This means that there is no place in scripture where a father is to be glorified, other than the heavenly father. For that religious group that talks much about their heavenly father with many wives that will people a new planet, (and in some of their theology they claim justifiable polygamy) the concept is totally against what the Bible teaches. The term "father" is used hundreds of times in scripture but almost always it is with regard to the heavenly father, from whom all wisdom and agape love comes, and who saves us by his grace, which is totally unmerited by us. "And do not call anyone on earth 'father', for you have one Father, and he is in heaven." (Matthew 23:9.) At the present time a homosexual man can be seen in the figure of a father image particularly if there is a single parent who is a mother in a divorce family relationship.

Another difficulty is that in many cultures the father has a different relationship to the family than the relationship that we have within the context of the Christian religion. He is an untrustworthy individual who is seen in a rather negative light. He is to be honored at the expense of the rest of the family. Such is not a true representation of the heavenly father who created, sustained and is involved in saving us for an eternal relationship. Such a relationship has just been completed in a trial in Canada.

A father became wealthy in his native Afghanistan and moved with his two plural wives and children to Canada. The girls responded to the culture in which they now lived by dressing appropriately for teen agers, and proceeded to acclimate to their environment, associating with and falling in love with other youth. The father claimed that by giving up their 'religious dress code' that they dishonored him, and his honor was more important than anything else to him. He projected a very deep religious feeling about the matter, but no remorse. The jury ruled that along with his son and his second wife, people pushed the car in which the three girls and the first barren wife were riding into a canal with their resulting death. Though the father claimed that he was innocent he repeatedly stated that it was God's judgment because they had ruined his honor.

Many of his religious inclination are moving to Canada, and also to the United States. Do such individuals follow the normal guide of the two democratic countries, and their Judeo Christian based moral code or do they follow their 'brought along' moral code?

This also means that there is no truth, biblically, to the life after death situation that when a man dies that he goes to a beautiful garden, with a flowing stream and has many maidens to satisfy his sexual desires. There is a vast number of people in the world who hold to this belief. The Bible again holds that the chief end of mankind is to glorify God and enjoy him forever. In the book of Hebrews we are reminded that there is a long line of believers who have faith, but that the faith they have is in a loving God who desires that all people should come to him in agape love as he has shown that love in Jesus the Christ. Again, that 'all' means the inclusion of homosexual or lesbian folk, created by God for life on the planet earth with the faith possibility of an eternal relationship with God the Father.

We believe and the Bible teaches that when we die the souls of believers go immediately to be with Christ and at Christ's return the bodies are raised to eternal life. Note that a body is a recognizable essence of the individual. The recognition may be the mannerisms of the person, as we recognize an individual by the way they walk, talk or relate to others. There are some things that we will not discover until that moment comes and that moment is a certainty. Christ's essence will probably be a bright and shining light and those who have had 'after life experiences' from which they returned, to human consciousness relate that they were greeted by such a bright light.

There are so many challenges that have yet to be accepted and met by a compassionately concerned Christian population. Now is the time for the homosexual and heterosexual citizens of the world to be of service to that world.

FINAL THOUGHTS

For a moment let's pause and review where we are. God showed in the Genesis chapters that he created mankind, both homosexual and also heterosexual and that it was good. He continues to create both and he still considers it good. Then we found that in Gomorrah the homosexual folk attempted to violate the heterosexual folks. That was a displeasure to God and so fire and brimstone rained down, which seems to be the horror of choice for the rest of the Bible. We talked about God creating nouns and that we have a freewill opportunity to choose (free will to use any verb we wish) what we want to do with those nouns, it is a verb reaction.

In the New Testament we found that Jesus never differentiated between the homosexual and the heterosexual person, both were sinners. There are many stories, parables that he used to list those problems that need correction, and sins that need forgiveness. Homosexuality is never listed in those lists, though some persons might consider the actions of homosexual persons to be immoral. There were no direct actions taken by homosexual persons in the New Testament. Again the Apostle Paul lists all sorts of sins, and is constant and consistent in listing circumcision in most of his letters along with immoral behavior, which is never defined along with other sins. Circumcision is used to show that a person can become a Christian without being circumcised. Then we came to Hebrews where for future generations circumcision, which includes the homosexual individual, is no longer a spiritual problem.

As we handled each book of the New Testament, we selected various passages that assist the Christian, in his or her spiritual growth. These passages are equally important to the homosexual person as well as the heterosexual person. No attempt has been made to group the passages into a particular theological pattern, as it is up to the individual Christian to do that as he or she sees fit. Some passages may seem new and others might be remembered from early Sunday School days. These passages, however, tell us we are saved by the grace of God, and salvation is not just for any special group or a specific cultural group, the socially elite, the wealthy or the impoverished, the heterosexual or the homosexual, or the females or the males. It is for all and it happens because God loves us and wants a relationship with us. Our only responsibility, as it comes in every gift, is to accept that salvation and thank him for it.

No doubt there are many who still feel that the actions of homosexual persons are immoral. It reminds me of the parable that Jesus told concerning the wheat and tares, found in Matthew 13:24-30. "Jesus told them another parable: 'The kingdom of heaven is like a man who sowed good seed in his field. But while everyone was sleeping, his enemy came and sowed weeds among the wheat, and went away. When the wheat sprouted and formed heads, then the weeds also appeared. The owner's servants came to him and said. 'Sir, didn't you sow good seed in your field? Where then did the weeds come from?' 'An enemy did this,' he replied. The servant asked him, 'Do you want us to go and pull them out?' 'No' he answered, 'because while you are pulling the weeds, you may root up the wheat with them. Let both grow together until the harvest. At that time I will tell the harvesters: 'First collect the weeds and tie them in bundles to be burned; then gather the wheat and bring it into my barn.'" I do not wish to infer that the homosexual folks are weeds, nor do I imply that the heterosexual folks who seek not to accept the homosexual folks are weeds.

This decision as to who is and who is not saved is totally up to God. We who live on the planet earth are to live life as closely as possible to that lived by Jesus the Christ, and to remember that his was a sacrificial existence. His life shows us a heavenly love in action and the wonder of the Bible is that we can through understanding the Biblical message effect change on our planet, earth. We believe that God's Holy Spirit works through us to effect this change.

The point is that wheat and the darnel, the weeds, are identical as young plants. They are wonderfully green shoots. It is only as they are old and ready for harvest that they are easily distinguishable. There are many who believe that homosexuals are the weeds and who say that we must judge them and keep out the weeds. But we do not have the power or the authority to judge. Regardless of whether the members, and pastors and elected leaders of the congregations are heterosexual or homosexual, God can and does work through thoroughly human persons. God is in charge and his Holy Spirit is totally active.

I am reminded of Galatians and the fifth chapter, and I find that all of the homosexual and heterosexual pastors that I know are the embodiment of the 22nd verse: "But the fruit of the spirit is love, joy, peace, patience, kindness, goodness, faithfulness, gentleness and self-control. Against such things there is no law. Those who belong to Christ Jesus have crucified the sinful nature with its passions and desires. Since we live by the Spirit, let us keep in step with the Spirit. Let us not become conceited provoking and envying each other." If there is any judging to take place it will be done by God, but in my best feelings they are wonderful folks.

Most of the homosexual pastors have had to endure rejection, something that Jesus had to endure from the religious leaders of his country, and they have made decisions under difficult circumstances. For years various theological segments of the denominations of the Christian church, who are honestly concerned about the purity of the church, have fought to keep homosexuals from serving as pastors and as lay leaders. It is a wonder that there are any who are still willing to take their spirit filled lives and risk them daily in a public witness, but we should remember as they do that they are witnessing to Christ not to themselves. Unfortunately when someone talks about immorality, the first thoughts that come to so many minds is, 'homosexual'. For many people this is going to have to be an "unlearned" thought, and prayer can help. Realistically, most live as pure a life style as they can under a pall of rejection. There is very little that we can tell them about unjust rejection that they have not already experienced.

Most have a deep desire for raising a family, and when possible they do have children. Most go through the process of adoption and often take children that are passed over because they may have defects, alcohol syndrome and other deficiencies. As I often tell children who have been adopted but who do not feel wanted, "There are many children that were accidents and not planned for and are a surprise to their parents, (ah, yes but still a joy) but with you, my adopted friend, your parents wanted you so much that they had to go through miles of red tape in order to secure you as a permanent member of their family."

Close friends of ours, two lesbians, wished to have children so one was artificially inseminated and ended up pregnant but with twins, a boy and a girl. They altered their schedules so that the children have much time with each of them. One of the first questions that they were faced with, by some of their friends was, "How are you two girls going to raise your son?" Without hesitation one said, "We have brothers who are manly men, who will be the father figures and make sure that the boy is well acclimated." Of course they could also have added that there are hundreds of thousands of single mothers who have sons and many of them do not have the resources of the four or five uncles. The twins will also have the help of several boy cousins, even of differing cultural patterns.

INSPIRATION PLUS A DETERMINATION

Now that the prelude is behind us, it is time to get down to business. "Hey, Ken what do you mean prelude, aren't you almost finished with the whole matter?" No Way! We have just begun. We've talked much about the past, what has happened, where scripture has led us, but my concern is the Holy Spirit of Almighty God, who is a wonderful source of strength, not to do my will, or our will but to do God's will on his planet, now.

For years in the Presbyterian denomination we voted at General Assemblies and in our Presbyteries on what role the homosexual folk would take in the affairs of our beloved Presbyterian Church, and we are neighbors to many other denominations who were and are still voting on similar measures. The Holy Spirit said, "Not yet," and we were like Paul who wanted to surge out of his location to overcome the world and the Holy Spirit said, "Not yet." Well, the time finally came when the Holy Spirit said, "Now is the time." Let me quote a poem to you, the source of which disappeared many years ago and I have not looked up for a long while.

"Somebody said that it couldn't be done

But he with a chuckle replied,

Well maybe it couldn't but he would be one

Who wouldn't say so 'til he tried.'

So he buckled right in, with a trace of a grin

On his face, if he worried he hid it,

And tackled the thing that couldn't be done

And believe it or not he did it."

We serve a mighty God and possibly it is time that we buckled right in with a trace of a grin. Never has the time been so right, the choices so obvious, and the presence of the Holy Spirit so 'plain as the nose on your face.' Might we say this is the time. Politically we face an uncertain future, and it really does not make a huge difference who wins the secular political election we are involved in, in spite of the candidates' glitz and glamour. I do wish that the money they are wasting on the TV ads was available to start water wells in Africa, or figure out how to get more rain, and that the kids in those countries might be fed so that they can be sharp when it comes time to figure out how their country is going to rebound.

We have experienced an Arab Spring, and too many think that it is just another time of the year. The spring I'm looking forward to is on the foot of each person in each one of those Middle East countries. At the present time the Christian folk of those countries are suffering persecution and where possible are moving out of the countries.

My hope is that they spring forward with a new measure of certainty. Likewise, I pray there is no war in Asia, especially one that decimates countries. We have countries that have massive armies and they are growing theirs while we, in our national life are cutting back. Then there are other places, with masses of folk and they must be involved in the world's affairs. They must also be involved in God's will that all may come to know him and glorify him.

Many of these places have already been introduced to the Word of God and it has simmered below the surface, hidden from political turmoil yet still awaiting a wakeup call by God's Holy Spirit. The Holy Spirit has been working mightily, continuing the work of many China Inland Missions and other mission groups.

And then there are the Koreans, who get up at 4 A.M. for prayer and study, to really start off the day on the right foot? Then we have folks in the provinces of Russia, the "Stans" who have experienced a new kind of love as missionaries head to the hinter land to bring modern conveniences and examples of God's love. They have experienced a new kind of love and they like it. And then there is an economic kind of spring where we finally admit that the world is in an economic mess.

And let's not forget that it is God's world. Regardless of how much millionaires have in the way of wealth and things, it is useless unless it is guided into those places where it is needed, and the need is by God's people all of whom we are. And now we have the inspiration of the Holy Spirit who can manage the whole effort. Never have we had more at our disposal, when it comes to the many "tower of Babel" languages, which we must translate into the Tower of Bible message.

Yes, and that translation has to be through our own minds and bodies, through our own efforts under the guidance of God's Holy Spirit for, "Now is the time for all good men to come to the aid of the countries", the most often typed phrase that was used for trying out all those typewriters, in the distant past and even now is used.

As I have many times read through the life of Jesus Christ, his message and his wandering into and through the lives of those who knew him, I am disturbed by the seemingly obvious fact that his problems were with the religious leaders. He did not fit the ideal that they had and they were unwilling for the most part to allow him to rule in their lives, and their judicatories, or courts. More than ever before do we need to read again the life of Jesus Christ, how he interacted with the common folk that he met while walking through that small district of Galilee and slightly beyond.

In one of my teen years my father said, "Ken, let's go upstairs into my bedroom, there are some things that I would like to tell you." Our house was crowded with people and his bedroom seemed the only quiet place. Immediately I thought, "Now I'm going to hear about the birds and the bees." Dad lay on one corner of the bed and I was on another. He had a pile of papers before him and they seemed to be the object of the talk I was about to hear.

He continued, "There are things that you should know as you grow up. Your mother and I have tithed all of our lives and we continue to tithe." At this time he was supporting two families and was working for a company that would soon fold. "I think that you should know how we tithe." He then explained that as he made more, that he gave more than the 'legal' tithe of ten percent. He said, "An offering isn't an offering until the tithe has been paid, but once it has been paid then the offering IS an offering." He may have made many other comments, often referring to the papers that lay between us but I'll never forget that day, and hence we in our family also tithe – plus.

But isn't it interesting that possibly ten percent of the population is homosexual or lesbian? And what have we done with that ten percent, that tithe of ten percent of the population, for many years? For much of that time many have argued about where they should fit, with many of us not wanting them to be part of us, not realizing that they not only fit in, they are a very important part of us. If the puzzle of the Christian churches looks a little strange at times, maybe it is because there are some pieces missing! We should not only welcome homosexuals but we should urge them to join with us in the great things that God is doing in the world and the even greater things that he will be doing in the near and distant future.

And let's not forget that it is God's Spirit who will oversee the "Eye in the Sky" effort. Wow, what a time to be alive. We have experienced years of planning, from the early Bible characters down to the modern times. It has taken four thousand years to get to this point where communication is electronically fast, and humanly warm. We are closer with the world than we ever had been and the Biblical message has been made loud and clear and pertinent to all cultures.

Of course there are many in the world who have yet to be introduced to the Holy Spirit. Some claim that he does not exist because they have not experienced him. You don't believe in the radio and TV waves? Well, turn on the radio or the TV and experience the wonder that many have yet to see and hear. The wonder of living under the influence of the Holy Spirit is way more real.

Have you listened to the folks who are trying to put into words and deeds, their thoughts concerning Arab Spring? They are screaming and throwing rocks, but what do they seek? What they are looking for is not Democracy, as some of them have been suffering under a form of it for a long while. What they are looking for is the Christian faith, the right of each person, man or woman, high cast or lowly peasant to develop and be used by God in the building of their country in his world. Each person is important, the women, more than chattel or objects of sexual predators. The children are important who will be challenged to strike out and serve others either less healthy, or more hungry for the world's goods, serving because their nation's children are carried on Christian shoulders.

And now we have the fervor and determination of the homosexual community. They have been serving others in their communities, often in selfless ways. They are intellectual, and many are under the guidance of the Holy Spirit, sometimes admitted and sometimes without realization. They have tremendous abilities and are capable of sharing the intense love they have with many others.

What do you see more than anything else on television? You see an announcer who says that he is going to tell you what has happened with regard to the weather. Then after a little bit of time he tells you after more news, what is happening with the weather. Then he tells you what is going to happen and then he or she tells you why it is going to happen and then he shows you pictures of what is out there and admits that it may not happen the way that he or she has decided, but something is going to happen. The Holy Spirit of God has that right and permission to do the same with respect to the inclusion of the homosexual persons into full membership of the ministry of the Church of Jesus Christ. Some great things are going to happen.

The prelude has been a stroll through the Old Testament and then the New Testament. We have been looking for where the Holy Spirit is acting and how we can be used. Our denominational predecessors have done a good job of spreading God's Word. They have not always answered all the questions, but they have prepared the people in the world to find the answers. We have been young birds and we are now prepared to fly out of the nest. But let me give some guidelines.

We have not talked about Gideon, (Judges 6:11) who was a commander of the Lord and was wise enough to listen to God. Even our military has begun to listen to Gideon. Gideon was told to pare down his Army, as though it was more trouble to control the army than it was to use them in military battle. So, if our army is small, or smaller, just remember that some of the countries of the world have tremendous armies. The political leaders in many countries will make sure that the military is fed first, as they depend upon them for security. The starving masses are thrown the crumbs, if there are any left. But wars are won how and where God decides. Jesus Christ was not worried about getting larger and larger crowds, but with the single individual. Often just a few missionaries sent to the remote country such as China have been responsible for the underground church that can so affect the world. Gideon reminds us to be ready to be of service, every day, in all the places that we travel and with all the folks we meet with all of our might for our might is the might of God.

Possibly one last word is in order concerning our homosexual friends and their service within our denomination and in the life of the Christian church. I have been aware of many church struggles. As a young person I was aware of the pastor of the Methodist Episcopal Church who spent much time with his youth. Several elderly women caused the District Superintendent to change our pastor's location. I remember the difficulty of the United Presbyterian Denomination, the Scotch Covenanters, of which we were a part uniting with the Presbyterian Church. I remember the Angela Davis affair and the anxiety that it caused, and also the uniting of the Southern Church with the Northern Church. We need more people of color to glorify God within the bounds of the black and white church. I was fortunate to be on the Synod Staff Personnel Committee at the time of the introduction of women ministers. Our next challenge appears to be the successful introduction of homosexual ministers into our denominational life.

Using our past experience with the introduction of woman ministers, I would recommend following a similar plan. We arranged with a church that had a vacant position, to place a woman minister in their church for a six month interim period. The Synod paid her salary. The first woman had to stay for the entire six months and as an interim she could not be called to the church she was serving. She took part in church, presbytery and synod activities and she had four calls when she completed her interim service.

Likewise, a second female minister spent six months and had several calls upon completion of her service. The barrier no longer existed. Possibly a similar situation could ease a newly ordained homosexual pastor into the denominational main stream of service.

By not accepting homosexuals we have restricted ourselves from at least ten percent of the population. That number is probably more when you consider the parents and family of the homosexual person, who know him or her as a loving member of their family. "What's the matter with the church?" has been stated by many folk. Again I am reminded that we are all saved by grace and that our purpose is to honor and glorify God and enjoy his presence. What the Bible does say and what it doesn't say seem entirely clear to me. Now is the time to accept fully and without reservation the homosexual population into our fellowships. Many of them have been trained through Sunday Schools, youth groups and regular worship preparing them for service in Christ's church. An acceptance of Jesus Christ as Lord and savior is the entry to a life and eternity, filled with excitement. May God bless us as we allow his presence into the lives of the church, and all of our members.

THE CONCLUSION OF THE MATTER

The church of Jesus Christ has gone through many stages of re-formation in its development. Actually much of the re-formation is rather a better understanding of the self-revelation of God through his Word and the work of the Holy Spirit. As the great head of the church, Jesus the Christ is also involved. God has always had a unique sense of timing and though we can experience him in our lives, through some of the miracles that Jesus Christ performed, it is also felt in his long-term, dealing with his people.

Possibly the first great step in re-formation was the understanding that worship included a self-sacrificial living of the created human being. That sacrificial living usually meant that something of great importance to the human being was 'given' to God so that we could share God's presence. Sometimes that which was given to God was the individual person, the ultimate gift. That does not mean a self-destruction, but is rather an acknowledgement that God is God of the universe, anything that we can know, and that which we do not know. It all still comes under the authorship of God.

Jesus Christ the son of God is positively an example of God giving something to mankind that was very close and precious to himself, as an example of this relationship. From this moment on, Jesus the Christ is involved in each of the steps necessary to draw nearer to God through the steps.

The next important step is for mankind to live according to the spiritual and the physical laws that God has instituted. This enables people to come into a more direct contact with God, always acknowledging God as supreme, but also following his lead in worship and in getting along with each other. The coming of Jesus Christ also had the purpose of clarifying the spiritual laws. Whereas we had words, now we have an example. Jesus did not change the laws, but made them visible to mankind, also an act of clarification of the existing laws. Now they 'make sense' when seen through the life of Jesus the Christ and his words and wisdom.

God's gift to the New Testament church was first the religious witness of the Old Testament's persons and the Ten Commandments, and then Jesus the Christ. The greatest gift is Jesus the Christ God's son, who is a constant and consistent gift.

Jesus Christ came to show how Godly living can be accomplished on the planet earth, or wherever mankind might go. He also lived and taught that God is constant and that the purpose of mankind is to honor and glorify God and to enjoy him forever. Christ becomes a conduit or a can-do-it to the presence of God the Father. Once entered into the spiritual family one continues to grow or die. It is true of plant life, animal life and human life, both physical and spiritual.

Next was an understanding that this new church was to be a fellowship of humans dedicated to glorifying God and enjoying him and was not to be restricted to the people of Israel. All cultures and people of varying colors were not only invited but urged to come into the fellowship. That meant that cultures long devoid of the awareness of God would have their cultures changed by seeing them through the, "Love God and glorify him eternally."

Another change came when it was understood that women had just as much right of determination to be children of God as did men, and that it was not necessary for men to be present for God to recognize women. That recognition of woman meant that women were also placed in positions of leadership and not only their learned wisdom but also their inherited selfless love-giving were an integral part of the message of God to the civilization of all people. Down into our time there are still those who follow their culture in preference to new spiritual revelations and there are still a vast number of folks who feel that women should not have a place of leadership.

A change in this area also came in the realization that each human is responsible for each other human. Not only is that responsibility a physical responsibility but also a spiritual responsibility. Though cultures do change, the message of God does not change. Cultures find new ways of showing the glorification to God but there may be cultural changes that do take place. Old mores have to be re-evaluated by the new awareness of God's love, the newly acquired teaching of Jesus and his life lived sacrificially so changes would be made.

Another change came when it was acknowledged that there were homosexual persons, of both sexes, throughout the cultures who were also equal in the mind of God as persons who likewise honored and glorified God. Though possibly not understood, the validity of their presence and sexual orientation did not inhibit or restrict them, but rather that their homosexuality was another means of glorifying God and to restrict it was to restrict that glorification.

And so we arrive at the present place of history, his-story. Each change or new revelation caused concern as they happened. It seemed that to those affected what had gone before became invalid when the new form or understanding of the reality of the new form emerged. It was understood that the new form was an intricate and valid expression of glorifying God and enjoying him. Each change or orientation is rather a building block upon which the new realization of God's glory and intense love for each human is shown in a new way.

The purpose of these rules is not just to live together but also to live as God's children, so that we can continue to honestly honor and glorify God. In that way we will enjoy not only his presence but the presence of each other in our fellowship, not only here on the planet earth but also into an eternal relationship with God the Father,

Even in modern times there are those who feel that heterosexual orientation is the only true orientation. However, the church soars on the winds of opposition. Time has been found to be the healer of all wounds and occasionally the wounding of all healers. The process and progress begun with Abraham who followed his father in a call to move west and become the leader of all people; that process and progress continues. Again, the ultimate purpose is to Glorify God and enjoy his presence. We can imagine that when Christ was on the cross that both he and his Father did not enjoy that fact. There is a joy expressed in Christian worship, however, that God is ultimately in charge and there is joy in that which will ultimately count. For emphasis I repeat, God is ultimately in charge, it is his world and we are his people.

THE CONTINUATION

We likewise find a continuum of resistance to change. The nations that surrounded Israel did not appreciate the intrusion into their cultures or their geographic area, and they still don't. Jesus the Christ found instant opposition when the leaders of Israel discovered his expressed desire to live strictly according to the spiritual law. The members of the young church found opposition everywhere they went, the acceptance for God the Father found almost an instant creation of a God who was superior in the eyes of their specific followers who numerically have populated the planet, to the God of Creation and salvation.

READER PARTICIPATION

Well, dear reader I am pretty much finished with my part. How have you come with your part? Remember, I left the larger than normal white spaces so that you could write down your questions, emphases or total disagreements or possibly even agreements, and find them when you went over them at the end of the book, and that is where we are. I also included each scripture location so that you could view it for possible further consideration. Ah, yes, and remember that my criterion is that each person planted on the planet earth should come to the place where he or she honors and glorifies God and therefore enjoys that relationship, as does God. Yes, I mean each individual regardless of sexual orientation, cultural tradition or learning or lack of learning.

I must also confess that I did go over each passage to make sure that it said what I think that it said, and hopefully my exegesis was sufficient. For the untrained theologian, exegesis is examining a word or phrase using other commentaries. I have eight single volume commentary series. I must admit that I would probably flunk Hebrew and possibly Greek if I were to enroll in a class now, at this end of my ministry. I wish that I had had books, with wide margins in the hundreds that I read during my preparation for ministry, and also during my ministry and also since my ministry. I did keep track of the theologically-related books that I read during my ministry as I was not adjacent to a theological library and for the most part my reading was of commentaries. Alaska and Hawai'i are not known for their theological libraries.

I anticipate that you probably have not agreed with me or with some of the conclusions that I have reached and so now is the time to review your disagreements, to think back over your preparation, cultural, religious and social to the present time. What questions did you have that you stated in the provided spaces?

There is of course a negative possibility to that which I have written. To be honest I can suggest a few.

1. **Why is it necessary to have gay rights demonstrations?** And it has a fairly calm answer, because they have been denied rights for so long that the only way they can be seen and known is through the demonstration avenue. I predict that there will be fewer demonstrations as more rights, to normalcy are granted.

2. **But the sexual part is so difficult to accept!** Have you ever watched a prostitute ply her trade? It is totally repulsive. What the average person does not realize is that the sexual part is not the only thing that makes the homosexual person different. They really are unique persons; keen, sensitive and community--concerned, whether their own community or larger community. And, they are willing to share these talents with others, and to use those talents to assist or help others.

3. **Are our children safe with them?** Yes and of course that question could also be applied to the heterosexual person. How safe are our children with persons who have a sick attitude concerning heterosexual behavior. Look back to the introduction. There were seven boys in my family and my parents felt totally safe with Dick Siebold being there. He was a super positive person and there was never an inkling of worry about him being with any one of us.

4. **What about the sexual deviate?** And of course that question applies to both homosexual and heterosexual folk, also. Yes, there are folks whose attitudes are repulsive and society has to deal with them, regardless of their sexual orientation. Of course that was a problem in Paul's day.

5. **Are there really 10 percent of the population, who are homosexual?** I have run no studies and have only the words of the homosexual folk to go by. I do know that there were several in the congregations that I served who were homosexual, but who would not declare that fact as they did not want to seem different. It is a totally moral behavior and they are just as concerned when one of them goes out of bounds. I must confess that once they are known, that your relationship does not even include the word homosexual, they are just wonderful persons with whom you are friends. They are totally dependable, totally friendly and totally willing to do just about any task to which they are assigned, and they do those tasks not only willingly but also eagerly.

6. **Why are they different?** You are going to have to ask God that question and as you are a created person, as are they, God does not have to answer you. God loves them and he sent his son to die for them, for all of us.

A FEW ADDITIONAL THOUGHTS

It has been this author's observation that those groups most opposed to the total acceptance of the homosexual person are religious groups, probably numbering four. These practice evangelism by population explosion, determining that in spite of the world's population explosion larger families mean more members of each group's adherents. They seek ever larger families, even though there will be problems finding adequate jobs and housing. The leadership of some of those groups is totally celibate and women do not have an equality of position within those groups. There is a movement toward total equality in some of those groups, but fundamentally women count for little more than a means to increase the number of adherents through having more and more children, or they provide a sexual expression for the males in the group.

How best to welcome the homosexual folks into your fellowship? For a long time, and still in some areas, there is extreme pressure for exclusion of the homosexual person. Therefore our welcoming has to be slow and totally honest and genuine. Our welcoming is not to increase the number of adherents but rather to open to those persons that favorite slogan of mine, "glorifying God and enjoying him forever."

Way back in Exodus the Ten Commandments, or should I say God's Very Strong Suggestions, began with a relationship to God the creator and sustainer of mankind. It is that relationship which I wish for every person, one of whom is the homosexual person. And, as the sun (God's love) shines through the rain (our troubled past) so we will behold the rainbow. They need no special programs, just a total acceptance of themselves into the life of the congregation, as you would every other person.

FINAL CONCLUSION

They started after supper on Friday. The father could not afford to miss a day of work. Immediately they felt the full force of a "Buffalo Blizzard" as wet snow-laden winds blew off of Lake Erie, cutting visibility down to almost nothing. The snow-belt lived up to its name. A mesmerizing-moving blanket of snow kept blowing from right to left obscuring anything that would indicate the road. Terror gripped the boy as he watched 'nothingness' come and go. Yet the father hummed as he steered the car, particularly looking out for stalled cars. But still the terror in the boy grew as he thought of all the possibilities: getting stuck in the ditch and freezing to death, hitting a parked car, plunging off the side of the road down an embankment, being hit by a truck from behind. The possibilities were endless and the thickening swirling mass of white only added to the anxiety of the moment. An uncle had died, the father and twelve year old son would represent the family and would leave for the Saturday morning funeral after supper on Friday night. It was a five hour drive from the small town near Buffalo, New York to Pittsburgh, Pennsylvania. Storm warnings were up for the route they would follow, west to Erie, Pennsylvania and then south through the mountains to Pittsburgh.

The car was a 'fairly new' Buick coupe, specially fitted with an extra 30 gallon tank where the luggage was usually stored. (the father did a lot of driving and worked for a gasoline company). This often brought chuckles, when the gas station attendant kept pouring gas in after most cars would have been filled. There was comfort in the big snow tires, immediately under that big tank.

Finally, realizing the terror in his son the father explained, "Son, relax. I have driven this road many times and I know it well."

"But Dad, how can you see where you are going?"

"Well, son, I know that all those telephone poles are on the left hand side of the road. As long as I stay to their right and watch for parked cars we are safe and soon we will be out of the snow. I trust God. You move over here, snuggle up to me, trust me and wait and see."

When I awoke it was to the hum of snow tires on wet pavement. The snow was gone and Pittsburgh was only an hour away. I did not realize then the worries that passed through my father's mind: the support of two families, a total of twelve persons, caused by a brother-in-law's death, the impossibility of his gasoline department's supporting a company that had financially gone bankrupt and would soon cause his unemployment, an expanding world war that would take all of his sons and nephews but not return his eldest son. But I did know that my father had a faith that was visible, verbal and vital.

I'm now older than my father was at the time of the "Blizzard of '39", and have passed through many blizzards of my own, the loss of a son and brothers as well as parents, ridiculed often for following a life style out of step with modern society, having to deal lovingly and rationally with occasionally irrational and unloving folk. I've had hurricanes of demands for time, talent and testing; walking a tightrope with three sides, fitting in more hours of work than there are hours in a day, expected to be all things to all people when they do not know what it is that they want, attempting to meet the needs of a society that has gone berserk in its demands, but which has flinched and withdrawn from meeting its obligations.

I still have many questions and fears concerning the homosexual folks whom I call my friends, and also family. There are heterosexual folks who are jealous of the close feelings that homosexual folk have for each other. If God was really concerned about homosexual folk, why does he continue to create them? What is his special will for them in this confused world? How can I quit being reactive and become proactive with respect to the inclusion of homosexual folk in the life of the church? Is the problem the homosexual folk or our feelings about them? When was the last time that I invited homosexual folk into the worship experience of my church? How can I find their experience and expertise and involve them in the life of my worshipping group?

I don't know how God will solve the problems, but he will. Through it all, comes the remembrance of that Buick coupe and watching the face of my father as he searched for stalled cars and watched the telephone poles on the left hand side of the road, plowed through that moving blanket of snow and exercised his faith in his heavenly Father.

And I hear my heavenly father say, "Son, I have traveled this way often and I know the road. You snuggle up to me and trust me and rest and soon this blizzard will be over and things will be fine. "

Each of us has storms that we meet regularly. My father's words, as well as my Heavenly Father's words, are still valid, "You snuggle up to me and trust me and rest and soon this storm will be over." We may not know the future, but He does so let's just continue on to our goal, to glorify God and enjoy him forever.

Let us close in prayer. "Gracious God, we thank you for the lives that you have given us, for the close love relationships that we feel for one another and particularly that we feel toward you. Help us to strengthen our love relationships for all of your children. May we be used to bring peace and spiritual and physical sustenance to all of our neighbors, from my right hand side until it returns to my left hand side. We pray as humble persons, your creation, but at the same time sensitized by your Holy Spirit. We thank you for your son Jesus, our savior, not just for our sakes but for the sakes of everyone we meet. This we pray in his name. Amen."

OTHER BOOKS BY KEN SMITH

Judas A biographical novel.

    ISBN 0-595-16612-1

Parables from Paradise Parables from Hawai'i.

    ISBN 0-595-19659-4

Dick And Jane Marriage discussion with youth and others.

    ISBN 0-595-21542-6

S'more Parables From Paradise Additional Hawaiian parables

    ISBN 0-595-30552-0

Polar State Parables Parables from Alaska

    ISBN 0-595-30642-X

Dear Timothy Additional instructions in ministry

ISBN 0-595-37348-8

Grocery Bag Parables Still more parables from Hawai'i

ISBN 0-595-37635-5

John, No Greater Prophet Biographical historical novel

ISBN 0-595-39774-3

The True Faith, And How I Found it Samuel McGerald Author

Republication of great grandfather's book.

ISBN 978-1-4196-7610-9

Sheldon Jackson Parables Parables from Alaska Mission School

ISBN 9o78-0-595-44748-0

Samoan Parables Parables from Western and American Samoa

ISBN 978-0-595-44752-7

James, Camel Knees Biographical Historical Novel, Jesus' brother

ISBN-0—595-48336-5

Inupiat Parables Parables from Olgoonik (Wainwright) Alaska

ISBN 978-1-4401-1310-9

Puget Sound Parables Parables from Northwest Washington State

ISBN 978-1-4401-6595-5

A Full Life In Sitka, Alaska Volume 1 Martin R. Strand, Sr. Author

Ken Smith was the editor of the series.

ISBN 978-1-4502-5051-1

Voices From The Sitka, Alaska Wordsmith Volume 2 Martin R. Strand and, Sr. Author

Ken Smith was the editor of the series.

ISBN 978-1-4502-6918-6

Transitions From The Sitka, Alaska, Wordsmith Volume 3 Martin R. Strand, Author

Ken Smith was the editor of the series.

ISBN 978-1-4502-8528-5

Out Of The Web, Prostitute Habilitation

ISBN 978-1-4759-1400-9